AEPA
91
92

Professional Knowledge – Elementary & Secondary
Teacher Certification Exam

By: Sharon Wynne, M.S
Southern Connecticut State University

"And, while there's no reason yet to panic, I think it's only prudent that we make preparations to panic."

XAMonline, INC.
Boston

To obtain permission(s) to use the material from this work for any purpose including workshops or seminars, please submit a written request to:

XAMonline, Inc.
21 Orient Ave.
Melrose, MA 02176
Toll Free 1-800-509-4128
Email: info@xamonline.com
Web www.xamonline.com
Fax: 1-781-662-9268

Library of Congress Cataloging-in-Publication Data

Wynne, Sharon A.
    Professional Knowledge – Elementary & Secondary 91, 92: Teacher Certification / Sharon A. Wynne. -2nd ed. ISBN 978-1-58197-291-7
    1. Professional Knowledge – Elementary & Secondary 91, 92   2. Study Guides.
    3. AEPA   4. Teachers' Certification & Licensure.   5. Careers

Disclaimer:
The opinions expressed in this publication are the sole works of XAMonline and were created independently from the National Education Association, Educational Testing Service, or any State Department of Education, National Evaluation Systems or other testing affiliates.

Between the time of publication and printing, state specific standards as well as testing formats and website information may change that is not included in part or in whole within this product. Sample test questions are developed by XAMonline and reflect similar content as on real tests; however, they are not former tests. XAMonline assembles content that aligns with state standards but makes no claims nor guarantees teacher candidates a passing score. Numerical scores are determined by testing companies such as NES or ETS and then are compared with individual state standards. A passing score varies from state to state.

Printed in the United States of America

AEPA: Professional Knowledge – Elementary & Secondary 91, 92
ISBN: 978-1-58197-291-7

TABLE OF CONTENTS

THIS PAGE BLANK

SUBAREA I.   STUDENT DEVELOPMENT AND LEARNING

COMPETENCY 1.0   UNDERSTANDS HUMAN DEVELOPMENTAL
                   PROCESSES AND VARIATIONS AND HOW TO USE
                   THIS KNOWLEDGE TO PROMOTE STUDENT
                   DEVELOPMENT.

**Skill 1.1   Identifies characteristics, processes, and progressions of
               students' cognitive, physical, motor, social, emotional, and
               language/communicative development**

The teacher should have a broad knowledge and thorough understanding of the development that typically occurs during the students' current period of life. More importantly, the teacher should understand how children learn best during each period of development. The most important premise of child development is that all domains of development (physical, social, and academic) are integrated. Development in each dimension is influenced by the other dimensions. Moreover, today's educator must also have knowledge of exceptionalities and how these exceptionalities affect all domains of a child's development.

Physical Development

It is important for the teacher to be aware of the physical stage of development and how the child's physical growth and development affect the child's learning. Factors determined by the physical stage of development include: ability to sit and attend, the need for activity, the relationship between physical skills and self-esteem, and the degree to which physical involvement in an activity (as opposed to being able to understand an abstract concept) affects learning.

Physical development for high school students involves a complexity of physiological and physical changes to the body and emotional states. Students in comprehensive high schools are being asked to engage in the educational process in a manner of maturity and scope that is sometimes beyond their capacity during a time of complicated physiological factors. The transition from childhood development to teenage development is a journey of physical growth and coordination. A teenager is who is making that transition is also working to acclimate to the physical demands of a comprehensive educational expectation that will ultimately impact the rest of his/her future livelihood.

Cognitive (Academic) Development

Children go through patterns of learning beginning with pre-operational thought processes and move to concrete operational thoughts. Eventually they begin to acquire the mental ability to think about and solve problems in their head because they can manipulate objects symbolically. Children of most ages can use symbols such as words and numbers to represent objects and relations, but they need concrete reference points. It is essential children be encouraged to use and develop the thinking skills that they possess in solving problems that interest them. The content of the curriculum must be relevant, engaging, and meaningful to the students.

Piaget, child development theorist would say that teenagers are in an operational stage of development that is fully functional in cognitive thought and actions. As children get older, their capacity to totally integrate their learning experiences and life experiences into a global vision creates a foundation of learning. Students are now constructivist thinkers who can construct new learning opportunities from the world around them. The process of critical thinking skills and problem solving skills that students must use during the high school years to navigate through the maze of academic and social expectations is crucial during these cognitive years of development.

Social Development

Children progress through a variety of social stages beginning with an awareness of peers but a lack of concern for their presence. Young children engage in "parallel" activities, playing alongside their peers without directly interacting with one another. During the primary years, children develop an intense interest in peers. They establish productive, positive, social, and working relationships with one another. This stage of social growth continues to increase in importance throughout the child's school years including intermediate, middle school, and high school years. It is necessary for the teacher to recognize the importance of developing positive peer group relationships and to provide opportunities and support for cooperative small group projects that not only develop cognitive ability but also promote peer interaction. The ability to work and relate effectively with peers is of major importance and contributes greatly to the child's sense of competence. In order to develop this sense of competence, children need to be successful in acquiring the knowledge and skills recognized by our culture as important, especially those skills which promote academic achievement.

The social stages of development for older students encompass a different complexity of peer relationships. Students are beginning to discover their self-identity and self in terms of peers. The judgment of peers creates an emotional instability and imbalance during the middle and high school years that can derail the best laid plans for students aspiring to meet specific academic and behavioral goals and objectives.

Skill 1.2   Recognizes ways in which a student's development in any domain (e.g., cognitive, social, language/communicative) may affect performance in other domains.

Adolescence is a complex stage of life. While many people joke about the awkwardness of adolescence, it is particularly important to remember that this stage of life is the stage just before adulthood. While people do indeed develop further in adulthood, the changes are not as quick or significant as they are in adolescence.

When we say that development takes place within domains, what we mean is simply that different aspects of a human change. So, for example, physical changes take place (e.g., body growth, sexuality); cognitive changes take place (e.g., better ability to reason); linguistic changes take place (e.g., a child's vocabulary develops further); social changes take place (e.g., figuring out identity); emotional changes take place (e.g., changes in ability to be concerned about other people); and moral changes take place (e.g., testing limits).

The important thing to remember about adolescent development within each of these domains is that they are not exclusive. For example, physical and emotional development are tied intricately, particularly when one feels awkward about his or her body; or when emotional feelings are tied to sexuality; or when one feels that he or she does not look old enough (as rates of growth are obviously not similar). Moral and cognitive development often goes hand in hand when adolescents rationalize their behavior or search for role models.

What do educators need to know about this? Well, first, it is important to be sensitive to changes in adolescents. Just because you see a change in one area does not mean that there aren't bigger changes in another area, hidden beneath the surface. It is also important to realize that adolescents may be deeply hurt over certain issues that may or may not be directly related to the changes they are going through. Educators should always be on the lookout for signs of depression, drug use, and other damaging activities, behaviors, or symptoms.

Understanding the impact of cognitive, social and communicative skill processing is imperative in furthering the acquisition of learning. Students who have a network for collaborative support in the classroom must have a diverse circle of systems in place that could be defined in the following Figure 1.

Figure 1

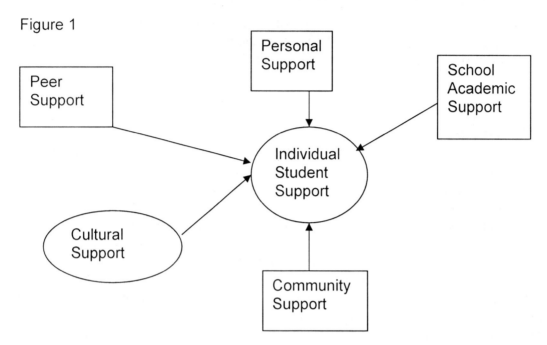

In Figure 1, the individual learner is the center of the networking that includes peer, personal, school and community support. Students who are directly impacted by family and peer support are typically being manipulated by the interrelationships and judgments that direct their social and cognitive attitudes and behavioral input in the classroom. Students can directly impact their own academic success in a positive manner by networking constructively within the educational community. Students can perceive and interpret community support as a support system or as a stress on their academic and cognitive development.

An effective support system includes a multitude of networking systems that play integral roles in assisting student learning objectives and goals. Cultural support will prevent generalizations of other cultures and provide sharing of one's own cultural stories and identity. For example, Nick Jones, an African American 10th grade student who is a star basketball player and a mediocre student, would need the network support system to intervene and help him prioritize academic success as a primary goal with basketball as a secondary outcome of high school success. Nick's cultural, family and community support teams would be integral in creating needed input for reorganizing Nick's attention to developing a sound academic portfolio, along with an A+ dunk during a basketball game.

Skill 1.3   Demonstrates knowledge of how specific developmental factors may affect learning.

Students at the middle level are continually undergoing physical and emotional changes and development. No matter how well we might try to prepare them for this, they have no point of reference within their own life experiences. Everything that is occurring is new and unfamiliar to these students, and often makes them uncomfortable about themselves. Often these physical, hormonal and emotional changes will occur in spurts, moving some ahead of their peers, in general, and leaving some behind. In most cases, the individual feels different and often is treated as different by his or her peers. The student may feel socially awkward, and this may be reflected in schoolwork and especially in classroom participation. The teacher must be sensitive to the issues of a developing child and aware of the impact this may have on student learning, classroom decorum and the cohesion among classmates, which the teacher is trying to foster.

The teacher of students in later childhood and early adolescence should have a broad knowledge and understanding of the phases of development which typically occur during this stage of life. And the teacher must be aware of how receptive children are to specific methods of instruction and learning during each period of development. A significant premise in the study of child development holds that all domains of development (physical, social, and academic) are integrated. Development in each dimension is influenced by the others. Equally important to the teacher's understanding of the process is the knowledge that developmental advances within the domains occur neither simultaneously nor parallel to one another, necessarily.

It is important for the teacher to be aware of the physical stages of development and how changes to the child's physical attributes (which include internal developments, increased muscle capacity, improved coordination, hormonal imbalances, awakening sex drive and other attributes as well as obvious growth) affect the child's ability to learn. Factors determined by the physical stage of development include: ability to sit and attend, the need for activity, the relationship between physical coordination and self-esteem, and the degree to which physical involvement in an activity (as opposed to being able to understand an abstract concept) affects learning and the child's sense of achievement.

Early adolescence is characterized by dramatic physical changes moving the individual from childhood toward physical maturity. Early, prepubescent changes are noted with the appearance of secondary sexual characteristics. Girls experience a concurrent rapid growth in height, which occurs between the ages of about 9.5 and 14.5 years, peaking somewhere around 12 years of age. Boys experience a concurrent rapid growth in height, which occurs between the ages of about 10.5 to 11 and 16 to 18, peaking around age 14.

The sudden and rapid physical changes that young adolescents experience typically cause this period of development to be one of self-consciousness, sensitivity and concern over one's own body changes, and excruciating comparisons between oneself and peers. Because physical changes may not occur in a smooth, regular schedule, adolescents may go through stages of awkwardness, both in terms of appearance and physical mobility and coordination.

The impact of these physical changes on individual students is to make them more self-aware, more self-conscious and more self-absorbed. Constant comparison with peers developing at different rates will cause many individuals to feel inadequate or inferior, at least at times. While remaining sensitive to the genuine, emotional response of early adolescents to changes they cannot control and do not fully comprehend, the teacher will find it necessary to be more proactive in bringing students out of themselves and becoming interactive participants in the classroom learning experience.

The developmental aspect for older students is more complicated in that physiological hormonal surges create active learning curves that are entangled in emotional and physical growth. In a typical high school classroom, students are energetic and driven by peer-interrelationships that are both constructive and destructive in their impact on students' current and future academic goals and aspirations.

Both teachers and students must understand that, as students struggle to navigate their way through the developmental changes that are not always aligned with the academic and behavioral expectations of the classroom, the journey is precarious. The social aspect of learning may often precede the academic expectations in high school classrooms. Student interactions are magnified during this time of developmental growth and the importance of academic learning is marginalized, in some cases, to the detriment of student academic performance and graduation.

Skill 1.4   Understands that developmental variations among students may affect instructional decision making in given situations

Knowledge of age-appropriate expectations is fundamental to the teacher's positive relationship with students and effective instructional strategies. Equally important is the knowledge of what is individually appropriate for the specific children in a classroom. Developmentally oriented teachers approach classroom groups and individual students with a respect for their emerging capabilities. Developmentalists recognize that kids grow in common patterns, but at different rates which usually cannot be accelerated by adult pressure or input. Developmentally oriented teachers know that variance in the school performance of different children often results from differences in their general growth. With the establishment of inclusionary classes throughout the schools, it is vital for all teachers to know the characteristics of students' exceptionalities and their implications on learning.

The effective teacher is cognizant of students' individual learning styles and human growth and development theory and applies these principles in the selection and implementation of appropriate instructional activities. Learning activities selected for younger students (below age eight) should focus on short time frames in highly simplified form. The nature of the activity and the content in which the activity is presented affects the approach that the students will take in processing the information. Younger children tend to process information at a slower rate than older children (age eight and older).

On the other hand, when selecting and implementing learning activities for older children, teachers should focus on more complex ideas, as older students are capable of understanding more complex instructional activities. Moreover, effective teachers select and present these activities in a manner consistent with the level of readiness of his/her students.

The effective teacher takes care to select appropriate activities and classroom situations in which learning is optimized. The classroom teacher should manipulate instructional activities and classroom conditions in a manner that enhances group and individual learning opportunities. For example, the classroom teacher can organize group-learning activities in which students are placed in a situation in which cooperation, sharing ideas, and discussion occurs. Cooperative learning activities can assist students in learning to collaborate and share personal and cultural ideas and values in a classroom-learning environment.

The effective teacher selects learning activities that will serve as a tool to reinforce the teacher's lesson presentation and will introduce the activities in a meaningful instructional sequence. Additionally, selected learning objectives should be consistent with state and district educational goals that focus on National educational goals (Goals 2000) and the specific strengths and weaknesses of individual students assigned to the teacher's class.

If an educational program is child-centered, then it will surely address the abilities and needs of the students because it will take its cues from students' interests, concerns, and questions. Making an educational program child-centered involves building on the natural curiosity children bring to school, and asking children what they want to learn.

Teachers help students to identify their own questions, puzzles, and goals, and then structure widening circles of experience and investigation of those topics. Teachers manage to infuse all the skills, knowledge, and concepts that society mandates into a child-driven curriculum. This does not mean that teachers are passive and respond only to students' explicit cues. Teachers also draw on their understanding of children's developmentally characteristic needs to design experiences that lead children into areas they might not choose. Teachers also bring their own interests and enthusiasms into the classroom to share and to act as a motivational means of guiding children.

Implementing such a child-centered curriculum is the result of very careful and deliberate planning. Well thought-out planning includes specifying behavioral objectives, specifying students' entry behavior (knowledge and skills), selecting and sequencing learning activities so as to move students from entry behavior to mastery of the objective, and evaluating the outcomes of instruction in order to improve planning.

Planning for instructional activities entails the selection of the activities the teacher and students will engage in during a period of instruction. Planning is a multifaceted activity which includes the following considerations:

- the determination of the order in which activities will be completed

- the specification of the component parts of an activity, including their order

- the materials to be used for each part, and the particular roles of the teacher and students

- decisions about the amount of time to be spent on a given activity and the number of activities to be completed during a period of instruction

- judgment of the appropriateness of an activity for a particular situation

- specifications of the organization of the class for the activity

Attention to the learner's needs during teacher planning is foremost and includes identification of the subject content area which the students already know or need to know. Matching learner needs with instructional elements (such as content, materials, activities, and goals) and the determination of whether or not students have performed at an acceptable level following instruction, are the ultimate goals of effective planning.

Teacher planning on the high school level is a collaborative process that involves extensive strategic instructional implementation. Most curriculums are developed from a cognitive and knowledge based modality where subject matter from previous years becomes building blocks for future years. For example, in a high school math class, students in a freshman class will take Algebra 1 in preparation for taking Algebra 2 as a sophomore and then taking Pre-Calculus as a junior.

High school curriculum is targeted towards a comprehensive educational base that is specific, and requires the demonstration of student learning on state and classroom assessments. In most states, high school sophomores are required to take a state assessment examination in math, writing and reading that determines whether they are performing and learning at standard or below standard. State testing has become a determinant of whether students are meeting academic expectations as defined by GLEs (Grade Level Expectations) and whether school districts are meeting the federal NCLB (No Child Left Behind) law or AYP (Adequate Yearly Progress).

Currently, student academic performance in school communities is directly tied to federal funding in school districts. Schools that are underperforming on assessment exams will fill the pinch of the marginalizing of federal funding for their districts, which ultimately impacts individual school buildings. There is an influx of millions of educational dollars to increase student achievement and performance on state assessment exams, so for districts nationwide, the trend is to create alternative curriculum and instructional implementation to address students who are identified as underperforming in classrooms.

Districts are beginning to recognize the huge impact of developmental variances of students in today's classrooms. Some students are developmental unprepared to work on the expected skill level of grade level course instructions. Concurrently, teachers are unprepared to instruct the variances of inadequate skill levels for district prescribed curriculum. Some teachers are unable to flex prescribed curriculum to fit student performance levels, so instructional decision-making is constantly compromised in the classroom.

Skill 1.5   Demonstrates knowledge of the importance of considering developmental characteristics of students when evaluating alternative instructional strategies.

The constructivist view of student learning asserts that the learner constructs knowledge through inquiry and application of learning. As a developmental characteristic of student learning, constructivism personalizes the meaning and acquisition of how students view their world. For teachers, the constructivist view increases the diversity of academic instructional tools in their tool-kits by allowing the teacher to see knowledge as emerging within the context of the academic curriculum.

Teachers further understand that if students are able to provide self reflecting reference points in the acquisition of knowledge, students will master the importance of subject matters and take learning seriously. The inquiry of the world around them provides students with a global learning classroom that generates a natural exchange of ideas and questions about the application of subject content matter from the classroom. Constructivism is real learning for teachers and students because it creates additional learning materials and problem solving issues for the classroom environment.

In the traditional classroom environment, the teachers construct instructional strategies and learning environments for classrooms and student interactions. The premise is that if the teacher has been instrumental in creating that effective learning environment, the student will learn in a productive manner. But if students are allowed to access their own knowledge base and build that base around teacher curriculum expectations, both students and teachers will experience an educational transformation in learning acquisition. Students will become more cognizant about their learning and better able to apply and synthesize that learning in the classroom.

Skill 1.6   Recognizes learning opportunities and environments that promote students' developmental progress.

Academic Expectations

In a document prepared for the Southern Regional Education Board, on "Strategies for Creating a Classroom Culture of High Expectations," Myra Cloer Reynolds summarized the process necessary to meet the stated objective when she wrote, "*Motivation and classroom management skills are essential to creating and sustaining an environment of high expectations and improvement in today's schools.*"

In some school systems, there are very high expectations placed on certain students and little expectation placed on others. Often, the result is predictable: you get exactly what you expect to get. And you seldom get more out of a situation or person than you are willing to put in. Teachers are expected to provide the same standards of excellence in education for all students. This standard cannot be upheld or met unless teachers have (and convey) high expectations for all students.

Considerable research has been done, over several decades, regarding student performance. Time and again, a direct correlation has been demonstrated between the teacher's expectations for a particular student and that student's academic performance. This may be unintended and subtle but the effects are manifest and measurable. For example, a teacher may not provide the fullest effort on behalf of the student when there are low expectations of success. And the student may "buy into" this evaluation of his or her potential, possibly becoming scholastically further burdened by low self-esteem. Other students, with more self-confidence in their own abilities, might still go along with this "free ride"--willing to do only what is expected of them and unwittingly allowing this disservice to hamper their academic progress.

There are a variety of ways in which a teacher can convey high expectations to students. Much has to do with the attitude of the teacher and positive interactions with the students—clearly stating expectations and reinforcing this at every opportunity.

- Notify the class of your high expectations for their academic success. Let them know that they will be able to acquire all the skills in which you will be instructing them, and you take personal responsibility and pride in their success.
- Speak to the class about the opportunity to support your goals for their success. Let them know that you appreciate having a student approach you with questions, problems or doubts about her or his performance. When you welcome student questions it enables you to help them directly, increasing their success and your success as a teacher
- Never lower standards or "dilute" instruction for certain students. It is the teacher's responsibility to ascertain the means to bring the student's academic performance up to standards
- Use all forms of teacher communication with students to reinforce your high expectations for them—as a class, and especially as individuals. What we internalize as individuals, we utilize in group settings.

An example of an opportunity to communicate expectations would be when writing comments on exams and papers being returned to individual students. You should provide positive reinforcement regarding the progress the student is making toward your high expectations for his or her academic achievement. If the work itself is below expectations—perhaps even substandard—provide positive, constructive comments about what should be done to meet your expectations. Express your confidence in the student's ability to do so. A negative comment, like a negative attitude, is unacceptable on the part of the teacher. The teacher may deem it necessary to speak one-on-one with the student, regarding his or her performance. Remember, however, no student ever feels motivated when reading the words, "<u>See me</u>," on an exam or assignment.

Developmental Responsiveness

Within the school system, administrators, faculty as a whole, and the individual classroom teacher strive to develop an environment which provides for personalized support of each student's intellectual, physical, emotional, social and ethical development. Members of the faculty and staff are assigned to provide mentoring, advice and advocacy in response to the varying needs of students during their educational experience. Along with in-house professionals who are prepared to meet the developmental requirements of a diverse student population, many school systems provide programs and individuals who reach out to parents and families and the community, on behalf of the students.

Curriculum is developed which is socially significant and relevant to the personal interests of students. Classroom teachers plan, prepare and deliver instructional modules which are directed toward specific issues of childhood development (physical, intellectual, emotional, etc.) and incorporate student participation in all related discussions and activities. Wherever possible, interdisciplinary instructional modules (devised, developed and presented by teachers from different disciplines,each providing his/her own skill sets to achieve comprehensive understanding of the subjects/issues) should be employed to provide the most efficient use of faculty resources and the most effective means of introducing the students to all aspects and skills related to a subject.

Equity

Equity in the learning community addresses the following issues:

- Equal Access
- Equal Treatment
- Equal Opportunity to Learn
- Equal Outcomes

Equal access requires that there be no impediment (physical, cultural, intellectual, social, economic, etc.) or bias which restricts some students from access which is available to others.

Equal treatment ensures that no student is valued above or below the others. Physical, intellectual, cultural, economic or other criteria may not be applied in determining how a student is treated. Equally high academic expectations are afforded all students, with the assurance that this objective is achievable and will be supported by the teacher and the educational system.

Equal opportunity to learn requires that every student have equal access to all resources, physical and intellectual as well as equal instruction and support from the classroom teacher and staff.

Equal outcomes require that instruction and evaluation are structured to ensure all students acquire the skills being taught.

While equal treatment and equal access for all individuals is mandated under various state and federal statutes, not every issue has necessarily been considered and addressed. There can be difficulties with interpretation of these statutes. There may be inconsistencies between the letter of the law and the intent of the law. Significant differences in the implementation and conduct of policy and procedure within institutions can also hamper the effectiveness of the laws and the intent with which these statutes were created. Equity may not be fully achieved if practices are instituted or changed superficially, only to comply with statutory regulations rather than internalized and embraced by the entire learning community as an opportunity to improve the educational system.

In an educational environment there should be no such impediments to achieving equity. The primary responsibility of every educator is to ensure that all aspects of the educational process, and all information necessary to master specified skills, are readily accessible to all students. There should be no conflict between laws mandating equity and educational philosophy. Policies, practices and procedures instituted to comply with (or surpass the requirements of) these laws support our educational objectives. By creating, internalizing and practicing the values of an academic culture with high expectations for all students and inclusion of all students in every aspect of the educational process, we provide for equity in education and fulfill our primary responsibility as educators.

COMPETENCY 2.0   UNDERSTAND LEARNING PROCESSES AND
STRATEGIES THAT PROMOTE STUDENT LEARNING
AND STUDENTS' ACTIVE ENGAGEMENT IN
LEARNING.

Skill 2.1   Demonstrates knowledge of learning processes (e.g., how
students construct and assimilate knowledge and develop new
skills.

There are several educational learning theories that can be applied to classroom
practices. Piaget developed an educational learning theory which defined four
learning stages: sensory motor stage (from birth to age 2); pre-operation stage
(ages 2 to 7 or early elementary); concrete operational (ages7 to 11 or upper
elementary); and formal operational (ages 7-15 or late elementary/high school).
Piaget believed children passed through these stages to develop from the most
basic forms of concrete thinking to sophisticated levels of abstract thinking.

Two of the most prominent learning theories in education today are brain-based
learning and the Multiple Intelligences Theory. Supported by recent brain
research, brain-based learning suggests that knowledge about the way the brain
retains information enables educators to design the most effective learning
environments. As a result, researchers have developed twelve principles that
relate knowledge about the brain to teaching practices. These twelve principles
are:
  • The brain is a complex adaptive system.
  • The brain is social.
  • The search for meaning is innate.
  • We use patterns to learn more effectively.
  • Emotions are crucial to developing patterns.
  • Each brain perceives and creates parts and whole simultaneously.
  • Learning involves focused and peripheral attention.
  • Learning involves conscious and unconscious processes.
  • We have at least two ways of organizing memory.
  • Learning is developmental.
  • Complex learning is enhanced by challenged (and inhibited by threat).
  • Every brain is unique.

*(Caine & Caine, 1994, Mind/Brain
Learning Principles)*

Educators can use these principles to help design methods and environments in
their classrooms to maximize student learning.

The Multiple Intelligences Theory, developed by Howard Gardner, suggests that students learn in (at least) seven different ways. These include visually/spatially, musically, verbally, logically/mathematically, interpersonally, intrapersonally, and bodily/kinesthetically.

The most current learning theory of constructivist learning allows students to construct learning opportunities. For constructivist teachers, the belief is that students create their own reality of knowledge and how to process and observe the world around them. Students are constantly constructing new ideas, which serve as frameworks for learning and teaching. Researchers have shown that the constructivist model is comprised of the four components:

1. Learner creates knowledge
2. Learner constructs and makes meaningful new knowledge to existing knowledge
3. Learner shapes and constructs knowledge by life experiences and social interactions
4. In constructivist learning communities, the student, teacher and classmates establish knowledge cooperatively on a daily basis.

When George Kelly (1969) stated that "human beings construct knowledge systems based on their observations" this paralleled Piaget's theory that individuals construct knowledge systems as they work with others who share a common background of thought and processes. Constructivist learning for students is dynamic and ongoing. For constructivist teachers, the classroom becomes a place where students are encouraged to interact with the instructional process by asking questions and posing new ideas to old theories. The use of cooperative learning that encourages students to work in supportive learning environments using their own ideas to stimulate questions and propose outcomes is a major aspect of a constructivist classroom.

The metacognition learning theory deals with "the study of how to help the learner gain understanding about how knowledge is constructed and about the conscious tools for constructing that knowledge" (Joyce and Weil 1996). The cognitive approach to learning involves the teacher's understanding that teaching the student to process his/her own learning and mastery of skill provides the greatest learning and retention opportunities in the classroom. Students are taught to develop concepts and teach themselves skills in problem solving and critical thinking. The student becomes an active participant in the learning process and the teacher facilitates that conceptual and cognitive learning process.

Social and behavioral theories look at the social interactions of students in the classroom that instruct or impact learning opportunities in the classroom. The psychological approaches behind both theories are subject to individual variables that are learned and applied either proactively or negatively in the classroom.

The stimulus of the classroom can promote conducive learning or evoke behavior that is counterproductive for both students and teachers. Students are social beings that normally gravitate to action in the classroom, so teachers must plan classroom environments that provide both focus and engagement to maximize learning opportunities. Designing classrooms that provide optimal academic and behavioral support for a diversity of students in the classroom can be daunting for teachers. The ultimate goal for both students and teachers is creating a safe learning environment where students can construct knowledge in an engaging and positive classroom climate of learning.

No one of these theories will work for every classroom, and a good approach is to incorporate a range of learning styles in a classroom. Still, under the guidance of any theory, good educators will differentiate their instructional practices to meet the needs of their students' abilities and interests using various instructional practices.

Skill 2.2   Recognizes strategies for facilitating learning in instructional situations (e.g., by building connections between new information and prior knowledge and experiences, relating learning to world issues and community concerns, by making learning purposeful)

First, teachers should realize that historically, there are two broad theories regarding the construction of meaning. One is behavioral learning. Behavioral learning theory suggests that people learn socially or through some sort of stimulation or repetition. For example, when we touch a hot stove, we learn not to do that again. Or, when we make a social error, and are made fun of for it, we learn proper social conventions. Or, we learn to produce something by watching someone do the same thing.

The other broad theory is cognitive. Cognitive learning theories suggest that learning takes place in the mind, and that the mind processes ideas through brain mapping and connections with other material and experiences. In other words, with behaviorism, learning is somewhat external. We see something, for example, and then we copy it. With cognitive theories, learning is internal. For example, we see something, analyze it in our minds, and make sense of it for ourselves. Then, if we choose to copy it, we do, but we do so having internalized (or thought about) the process.

Today, even though behavioral theories exist, most educators believe that children learn cognitively. So, for example, when teachers introduce new topics by relating those topics to information students are already familiar with or exposed to, they are expecting that students will be able to better integrate new information into their memories by attaching it to something that is already there. Or, when teachers apply new learning to real-world situations, they are expecting that the information will make more sense when it is applied to a real situation. In all of the examples given in this standard, the importance is the application of new learning to something concrete. In essence, what is going on with these examples is that the teacher is slowly building on knowledge or adding knowledge to what students already know. Cognitively, this makes a great deal of sense. Think of a file cabinet. When we already have files for certain things, it's easy for us to find a file and throw new information into it. When we're given something that doesn't fit into one of the pre-existing files, we struggle to know what to do with it. The same is true with human minds.

Skill 2.3   Recognizes how various teacher roles (e.g., direct instructor, facilitator) and student roles (e.g., self-directed learner, group participant, observer) may affect learning processes and outcomes.

The Teacher's Role

Teaching consists of a multitude of roles. Teachers must plan and deliver instruction in a creative and innovating way so that students find learning both fun and intriguing. The teacher must also research various learning strategies, decide which to implement in the classroom, and balance that information according to the various learning styles of the students. Teachers must facilitate all aspects of the lesson including preparation and organization of materials, delivery of instruction, and management of student behavior and attention. Simultaneously, the teacher must also observe for student learning, interactions, and on-task behavior while making mental or written notes regarding what is working in the lesson and how the students are receiving and utilizing the information. This will provide the teacher with immediate feedback as to whether to continue with the lesson, or if it is necessary to slow the instruction or present the lesson in another way. Teachers must also work collaboratively with other adults in the room and utilize them to maximize student learning. The teacher's job requires the teacher to establish a delicate balance among all these factors.

How the teacher handles this balance depends on the teaching style of the teacher and/or lesson. Cooperative learning will require the teacher to have organized materials ready, perhaps even with instructions for the students as well. Direct instruction methods will require the teacher to have an enthusiastic, yet organized, approach to the lesson. When teaching directly to students, the teacher must take care to keep the lesson student-centered and intriguing while presenting accurate information.

The Student's Role

Like the teacher, the student has more than one role in a child-centered classroom. In collaborative settings, each student is expected to participate in class or group discussions. Through participation, students begin to realize their contributions have a place in a comprehensive discussion of a topic. Participation engages students in active learning, while increasing their self-confidence as they realize their ideas are necessary for group success.

Students also play the role of observer. As previously stated, behavioral theorists believe that through observation, a human's mind begins to make sense of the world around them as they decide to mimic or avoid certain behaviors. In a classroom, students gain many positive outcomes from questioning, discussion and hands-on activities.

An important goal for students should be to become self-directed in their learning. Teachers help students obtain this goal by providing them with ample opportunities to seek out their academic interests with various types of projects and assignments. Self-directed learners gain a lot from their inquiries since the topic usually interests them, and when students take over certain aspects of their own education, they gain a sense of empowerment and ownership over their learning. This is an important role in the classroom because the sense of ownership promotes a sense of lifelong learning in students.

| Skill 2.4 | Recognizes effective strategies for promoting independent thinking and learning (e.g., helping students develop critical-thinking, decision-making, and problem-solving skills; enabling students to pursue topics of personal interest). |

Critical thinking helps students sustain learning in specific subject areas that can be applied within other subject areas. For example, when solving a math word problem on how much fencing material is needed to build a fence around a backyard area, a math student must understand the order of numerical expression to simplify algebraic expressions. Teachers can provide instructional strategies that show students how to group the fencing measurements into an algebraic word problem that with minor addition, subtraction and multiplication can produce a number equal to the amount of fencing materials needed to build the fence.

Since most teachers want their educational objectives to use higher level thinking skills, teachers need to direct students to these higher levels on the taxonomy. Questioning is an effective tool to lead students to these higher levels.

Low order questions are useful to begin the process. They insure the student is focused on the required information and understands what needs to be included in the thinking process. For example, if the objective is for students to be able to read and understand the story "Goldilocks and the Three Bears," the teacher may wish to start with low order questions (i.e., "What are some things Goldilocks did while in the bears home?" [Knowledge] or "Why didn't Goldilocks like the Papa Bear's chair?" [Analysis])

Through questioning, the teacher can control the thinking process of the class. As students become more involved in the discussion they are systematically being lead to higher level thinking.

- If Goldilocks had come to your house, what are some things she may have used? [Application]

- How might the story be different if Goldilocks had visited the three fishes? [Synthesis]
- Do you think Goldilocks was good or bad? Why? [Evaluation])

Various studies have shown that learning is increased when the teacher acknowledges and amplifies student responses to questions. For example, the teacher takes one student's response and directs it to another student for further comment. When this occurs, the students acquire greater subject matter knowledge. This is due to a number of factors. One is that the student feels that he or she is a valuable contributor to the lesson. Another is that all students are forced to pay attention because they never know when they will be called on. This is known as group alert. **The teacher achieves group alert by stating the question, allowing for a pause time for the students to process the question and formulate an answer, and then calling on someone to answer.** If the teacher calls on someone before stating the question, the rest of the students tune-out because they know they are not responsible for the answer. Teachers are advised to alert the non-performers to pay attention because they may be called on to elaborate on the answer. Non-performers are defined as all the students not chosen to answer.

The idea of directing the student comment to another student is a valuable tool for engaging the lower achieving student. **If the teacher can illicit even part of an answer from a lower-achieving student and then move the spotlight off of that student onto another student, the lower achieving student will be more likely to engage in the class discussion the next time.** This is because they were not put "on the spot" for very long and they successfully contributed to the class discussion.

Additionally, the teacher shows acceptance and gives value to student responses by acknowledging, amplifying, discussing or restating the comment or question. If you allow a student response, even if it is blurted out, you must acknowledge the student response and tell the student the quality of the response. For example: The teacher asks, "Is chalk a noun?" During the pause time a student says, "Oh, so my bike is a noun." Without breaking the concentration of the class, the teacher looks to the student, nods and then places his or her index finger to the lips as a signal for the student not to speak out of turn and then calls on someone to respond to the original question. If the blurted out response is incorrect or needs further elaboration, the teacher may just hold up his or her index finger as an indication to the student that the class will address that in a minute when the class is finished with the current question.

A teacher acknowledges a student response by commenting on it. For example, the teacher states the definition of a noun, and then asks for examples of nouns in the classroom. A student responds, "My pencil is a noun." The teacher answers, "Okay, let us list that on the board." By this response and the action of writing "pencil" on the board, the teacher has just incorporated the student's response into the lesson.

A teacher may also amplify the student response through another question directed to either the original student or to another student. For example, the teacher may say, "Okay", giving the student feedback on the quality of the answer, and then add, "What do you mean by "run" when you say the battery runs the radio?"

Another way of showing acceptance and value of student response is to discuss the student response. For example, after a student responds, the teacher would say, "Class, let us think along that line. What evidence proves what Jose just stated?"

And finally, the teacher may restate the response. For example, the teacher might say, "So, are you saying that the seasons are caused by the tilt of the earth?"

The teacher must maintain the focus of the classroom discussion on the subject matter by teacher-posed questions. When a student response is correct, it is not difficult to maintain academic focus. However, when the student response is incorrect, this task is a little more difficult. The teacher must redirect the discussion to the task at hand, and at the same time not devalue the student response. If a student is ridiculed or embarrassed by an incorrect response, the student may shut down and not participate thereafter in classroom discussion.

One way to respond to the incorrect answer is to ask the child, "Show me from your book why you think that." This gives the student a chance to correct the answer. Another possible response from the teacher is to use the answer as a non-example. For example, after discussing the characteristics of warm-blooded and cold-blooded animals, the teacher asks for some examples of warm-blooded animals. A student raises his or her hand and responds, "A snake." The teacher could then say, "Remember, snakes lay eggs; they do not have live birth. However, a snake is a good non-example of a mammal." The teacher then draws a line down the board and under a heading of "non-example" writes "snake." This action conveys to the student that even though the answer was wrong, it still contributed positively to the class discussion. Notice how the teacher did not digress from the task of listing warm-blooded animals; academic focus and the student's dignity were maintained.

It is more difficult for the teacher to avoid digression when a student poses a non-academic question. For example, during the classroom discussion of Romeo and Juliet, the teacher asks "Who told Romeo Juliet's identity?" A student raises his or her hand and asks, "May I go to the restroom?" The teacher could respond in one of two ways. If the teacher did not feel this was a genuine need, he or she could simply shake his or her head no while repeating the question, "Who told Romeo Juliet's identity?" If the teacher felt this was a genuine need, he or she may hold up the index finger indicating "just a minute," and illicit a response to the academic question from another student. Then, during the next academic question's pause-time, the teacher could hand the student the bathroom pass.

Using hand signals and body language to communicate with one student while still talking to the rest of the class demonstrates effective teacher "with-it-ness." "With-it-ness" is the behavior that demonstrates to the students that the teacher knows what he or she is doing. The teacher maintains academic focus with the class while attending to the needs of the one student who needs to use the rest room or go to the clinic. During the academic day, many non-academic tasks need to be done. If the students learn that the teacher is not sidetracked by these interruptions, they will stay on task and greater subject matter acquisition will occur.

The teacher may opt to ignore questions that are posed to throw the class off-task. For example, in response to an academic question the student asks, "What time does the bell ring?" The teacher may respond by shaking his or her head "no" and calling on someone else to answer the academic question. Under no circumstances should the student posing the non-academic question be given an answer. Otherwise, this is rewarding deviant behavior and will result in a loss of academic focus.

Teachers must avoid teaching tasks that fit their own interests and goals and instead design activities that address the students' concerns. In order to do this, it is necessary to find out about students and to have a sense of their interests and goals. Teachers can do this by conducting student surveys and simply by questioning and listening to students. Once this information is obtained the teacher can link students' interests with classroom tasks.

Teachers are learning the value of giving assignments that meet the individual abilities and needs of students. After instruction, discussion, questioning, and practice have been provided, rather than assigning one task to all students—teachers are asking students to generate tasks that will show their knowledge of the information presented. Students are given choices and thereby have the opportunity to demonstrate more effectively the skills, concepts, or topics that they as individuals have learned. It has been established that student choice increases student originality, intrinsic motivation, and higher mental processes.

The effective teacher uses advanced communication skills such as clarification, reflection, perception, and summarization as a means to facilitate communication. Teachers who are effective communicators are also good listeners. Teacher behaviors such as eye contact, focusing on student body language, clarifying students' statements, and using "I" messages are effective listeners. The ability to communicate with students, listen effectively, identify relevant and non-relevant information, and summarize students' messages facilitates establishing and maintaining an optimum classroom learning environment.

A classroom atmosphere that frowns on closed-mindedness and rewards openness to new and different approaches and ideas is powerful in shaping students' attitudes. Many of them will come from homes that practice narrow-minded judgmentalism and criticism of differences, so there will be obstacles. However, the classroom can be powerful in the development of children's future attitudes and philosophies.

If the teacher stays right on the cutting edge of children's experience, they will become more and more curious about what is out there in the world that they don't know about. A lesson on a particular country or even a tribe in the world that the children may not even know exists will reveal to them what life is like there for children their own age. In such a presentation, positive aspects of the lives of those "other" children should be included.

COMPETENCY 3.0 UNDERSTAND FACTORS THAT MAY AFFECT STUDENT DEVELOPMENT AND LEARNING, AND USE THIS KNOWLEDGE TO DESCRIBE LEARNING ENVIRONMENTS IN WHICH ALL STUDENTS CAN BE SUCCESSFUL.

Skill 3.1 Recognizes factors (e.g., social, emotional, cognitive, behavioral, physiological, gender, linguistic, environmental, familial, cultural, economic) that may affect students' development and learning.

Oftentimes, students absorb the culture and social environment around them without deciphering contextual meaning of the experiences. When provided with a diversity of cultural contexts, students are able to adapt and incorporate multiple meanings from cultural cues vastly different from their own socioeconomic backgrounds. Socio-cultural factors provide a definitive impact on a students' psychological, emotional, affective, and physiological development, along with a students' academic learning and future opportunities.

The educational experience for most students is a complicated and complex experience with a diversity of interlocking meanings and inferences. If one aspect of the complexity is altered, it may impact how a student or teacher views an instructional or learning experience. With the current demographic profile of today's school communities, the complexity of understanding, interpreting, and synthesizing the nuances from the diversity of cultural lineages could impede the acquisition of learning for students.

Teachers must create personalized learning communities where every student is a valued member and contributor of the classroom experiences. In classrooms where socio-cultural attributes of the student population are incorporated into the fabric of the learning process, dynamic interrelationships are created that enhance the learning experience and the personalization of learning. When students are provided with numerous academic and social opportunities to share their experiences, everyone in the classroom benefits from having an expanded viewpoint of the world.

Researchers continue to show that personalized learning environments increase the learning affect for students, decrease drop-out rates among marginalized students, and decrease unproductive student behavior that can result from constant cultural misunderstandings or miscues between students. When students are able to step outside their comfort zones and share the world of a homeless student or empathize with an English Language Learner (ELL) student who has just immigrated to the United States and is learning English for the first time, then students grow exponentially in social understanding and cultural connectedness.

Skill 3.2 **Recognizes how current and prior school experiences (e.g., teacher expectations, assessment practices) may affect students' perceptions, motivation, attitudes about learning, and performance.**

Teachers need to be aware that much of what they say and do can be motivating and may have a positive effect on students' achievement. Studies have been conducted to determine the impact of teacher behavior on student performance. Surprisingly, a teacher's voice can really make an impression on students. Teachers' voices have several dimensions—volume, pitch, rate, etc. A recent study on the effects of speech rate indicates that, although both boys and girls prefer to listen at the rate of about 200 words per minute, boys prefer slower rates overall than girls. This same study indicates that a slower rate of speech directly affects processing ability and comprehension.

Other speech factors such as communication of ideas, communication of emotion, distinctness/pronunciation, quality variation and phrasing, correlate with teaching criterion scores. These scores show that "good" teachers ("good" meaning teachers who positively impact and motivate students) use more variety in speech than do "less effective" teachers. A teacher's speech skills can have strong motivating elements. A teacher's body language has an even greater effect on student achievement and the ability to set and focus on goals. Teacher smiles provide support and give feedback about the teacher's affective state. A deadpan expression can actually be a detriment to the student's progress. Teacher frowns are perceived by students to mean displeasure, disapproval, and even anger. Studies also show that teacher posture and movement are indicators of the teacher's enthusiasm and energy, which emphatically influence student learning, attitudes, motivation, and focus on goals. Teachers have a greater efficacy on student motivation than any person other than parents.

Teachers can also enhance student motivation by planning and directing interactive, "hands-on" learning experiences. Research substantiates that cooperative group projects decrease student behavior problems and increase student on-task behavior. Students who are directly involved with learning activities are more motivated to complete a task to the best of their ability.

Young children believe that teachers have "eyes in the back of their head." The "with-it" teacher is truly aware of what the students are doing and sends this message to the students through his/her behavior. When a deviancy occurs in the classroom, the effective teacher knows which student(s) caused the deviancy and swiftly stops the behavior before the deviant conduct spreads to other students or becomes more serious.

The effective teacher demonstrates awareness of what the entire class is doing and is in control of the behavior of all students even when the teacher is working with only a small group of children. In an attempt to prevent student misbehaviors the teacher makes clear, concise statements about what is happening in the classroom directing attention to content and the students' accountability for their work rather than focusing the class on the misbehavior. It is also effective for the teacher to make a positive statement about the appropriate behavior that is observed.

The teacher must be careful to control the voice, both the volume and the tone. Research indicates that soft reprimands are more effective in controlling disruptive behavior than loud reprimands and that when soft reprimands are used fewer are needed.

The teacher who can attend to a task situation and an extraneous situation simultaneously without becoming immersed in either one is said to have "with-it-ness." This ability is absolutely imperative for teacher effectiveness and success. It can be a difficult task to address deviant behavior while sustaining academic flow, but this is a skill that teachers need to develop early in their careers and one that will become second nature, intuitive, and instinctive.

Verbal techniques, which may be effective in modifying student behavior and setting the classroom tone, include simply stating the student's name, explaining briefly and succinctly what the student is doing that is inappropriate and what the student should be doing. Verbal techniques for reinforcing behavior include both encouragement and praise delivered by the teacher. In addition, for verbal techniques to positively effect student behavior and learning, the teacher must give clear, concise directives while implying her warmth toward the students.

It is also helpful for the teacher to prominently display the classroom rules. This will serve as a visual reminder of the students' expected behaviors. In a study of classroom management procedures, it was established that the combination of conspicuously displayed rules, frequent verbal references to the rules, and appropriate consequences for appropriate behaviors led to increased levels of on-task behavior.

Skill 3.3   Recognizes the significance of the home environment (e.g., nature of the expectations of parents, guardians, or caregivers; degree of their involvement in a child's education) for student learning.

The student's capacity and potential for academic success within the overall educational experience are products of her or his total environment: classroom and school system; home and family; neighborhood and community in general. All of these segments are interrelated and can be supportive, one of the other, or divisive, one against the other. As a matter of course, the teacher will become familiar with all aspects of the system pertinent to the students' educational experience. This would include not only process and protocols but also the availability of resources provided to meet the academic, health and welfare needs of students. But it is incumbent upon the teacher to look beyond the boundaries of the school system to identify additional resources as well as issues and situations which will effect (directly or indirectly) a student's ability to succeed in the classroom.

Examples of Resources

- Libraries, museums, zoos, planetariums, etc.
- Clubs, societies and civic organizations, community outreach programs and government agencies can provide a variety of materials and media as well as possible speakers and presenters
- Departments of social services operating within the local community can provide background and program information relevant to social issues which may be impacting individual students, and can be a resource for classroom instruction regarding life skills, at-risk behaviors, etc.

Initial contacts for resources outside of the school system will usually come from within the system itself: from administration; teacher organizations; department heads; and other colleagues.

Examples of Issues/Situations

Students from multicultural backgrounds: Curriculum objectives and instructional strategies may be inappropriate and unsuccessful when presented in a single format which relies on the student's understanding and acceptance of the values and common attributes of a specific culture which is not his or her own.

Parental/family influences: Attitude, resources and encouragement available in the home environment may be attributes for success or failure. Families with higher incomes are able to provide increased opportunities for students. Students from lower income families will need to depend on the resources available from the school system and the community.

Family members with higher levels of education often serve as models for students, and have high expectations for academic success. And families with specific aspirations for children (often, regardless of their own educational background) encourage students to achieve academic success, and are most often active participants in the process.

A family in crisis (caused by economic difficulties, divorce, substance abuse, physical abuse, etc.) creates a negative environment which may profoundly impact all aspects of a student's life, and particularly his or her ability to function academically. The situation may require professional intervention. It is often the classroom teacher who will recognize a family in a crisis situation and instigate an intervention by reporting this to school or civil authorities.

Regardless of the positive or negative impact on the students' education from outside sources, it is the teacher's responsibility to ensure that all students in the classroom have an equal opportunity for academic success. This begins with the teacher's statement of high expectations for every student, and develops through planning, delivery and evaluation of instruction which provides for inclusion and ensures that all students have equal access to the resources necessary for successful acquisition of the academic skills being taught and measured in the classroom.

Skill 3.4   Recognizes how classroom factors (e.g., student-teacher interactions) may affect students' self-concepts and learning.

Teachers are role models in the classroom and facilitators of student learning. The student-teacher interaction is an integral component of whether a student will access educational content. Students who feel estranged from their teachers may have difficulty in academic acquisition of the subject area. As the adult role models in student lives during the bulk of their waking and working hours, teachers become the viable source of not only academic learning, but also life learning as well for students. Students are hypersensitive to teacher feedback and treatment in the classroom, so it is imperative that there exists a simpatico in the student-teacher relationship.

The classroom environment is the laboratory of student learning. In the classroom, the student will either feel safe and inclusive and able to become a productive contributor to his/her own learning or become disengaged from the learning process. Students feel a connection to teachers where there is trust and caring that is tangible and obvious. A teacher who stands outside the door to greet students entering the classroom provides an atmosphere of learning built on trust and caring that is tangible in the handshake and in the warm smile that says, "Welcome." Students want to feel understood and connected not only to their learning, but also to their teachers.

Quality time between teachers and students can directly impact a student's self-esteem and learning capacity. Students spend more time with teachers than with parents, so that adoration and bonding that happens at a core level will extend into areas of advice and counseling. As students struggle to understand their internal worlds, the struggles become manifest in their academic performance and behavioral expressions, both positive and negative.

A teacher's job is to listen to students and encourage them to problem-solve their own issues or take notes on outside referral information relevant to their problems. Teachers who can help students navigate the classroom environment successfully will make the greatest difference in the lives with their students. Personalizing the learning experience for students is about providing adult connections that communicate care and concern.

Teachers provide positive social reinforcers to create proactive student-teacher connections that may consist of words, a touch on the shoulder and facial expressions. Teachers use verbal reinforcers consistently as a system of behavior modification to reward students who are presenting on-task behavior in the classroom. For example, in a Language Arts classroom, the teacher says, "Okay, class, take out your Language Arts book." The teacher sees 1/3 of the class responding to the verbal directive; 1/3 of the class caught between compliance and social engagement and 1/3 totally ignoring the directive and continuing to talk. The teacher can pick out peer role models who are in compliance by saying "Thank you, Joe; great job on listening and following instructions." This verbal reinforcer may present a positive redirect for other students to comply with the original directive.

Teachers use lots of positive and proactive verbal reinforcers to modify student behavior in the classroom. A verbal example would be the following:

- Excellent job. Nice work. Great expression in your presentation. Perfect. I enjoyed your project presentation. Please share that thought with the class.

A nonverbal reinforcer would consist of the physical and visual demonstrations that exist in most classrooms between teacher and student:

- Direct eye contact, shoulder touch, proximity of where a teacher stands, head nod, smiles, wink, thumbs up sign, and a high five sign.

Graphic reinforcers are seen in marks on the paper: smiley faces, constructive comments, stars or stickers. Educators use graphic reinforcers worldwide to communicate effective work or work that needs serious improvement. In some classrooms, teachers provide tangible reinforcers or rewards that are considered extrinsic rewards for increased student academic or behavioral performances. High school classrooms may provide pizza parties as a transitional reward for reports that profile student academic achievement.

When a teacher has a relationship with a student that promotes trust and care, the teacher can help the student develop positive and proactive interactions in other areas. For example, if a teacher sees a student engaged in an argument with another student, the teacher could intervene in a manner that speaks of trust. The teacher can ask to speak privately with the student escalating the argument and explain to that student that his/her behavior is disruptive and could spiral into a more serious disciplinary offense. With trust, the student will listen and see the intervention as a helpful and thoughtful move from a teacher who truly cares about bringing out the best in his/her student, both academically and socially.

Skill 3.5   Identifies ways in which peer interactions may promote or hinder a student's success in school.

When organizing work groups in the classroom, the teacher should plan effectively to ensure productivity and avoid the following common pitfalls:
- One or two of the more vocal or energetic students dominate the group and virtually dictate the outcome of the process
- Other students, feeling left out or bored, detach themselves from the process, gain nothing from the experience, and may develop a negative attitude for the work, itself, or teamwork, in general.
- Given the opportunity to participate, some students refuse or avoid this out of shyness or a lack of interest in the topic or activity
- Even when individuals in small groups participate equally and evenly, presentation of their results to the entire class falls flat or becomes chaotic.
- There are no "born leaders" in the group and without constant supervision the members do nothing or resort to individual pursuits.

To prevent this, teachers should:

- Clearly define learning objectives for each group activity.
- Clearly define tasks that group members would need to accomplish to achieve the objectives.
- Set time limits—for total activity and for any linked segments.
- Predetermine how results of the groups' efforts will be reported to the teacher and/or the class and who will report what.
- Teach standards of conduct within the group
- Instill confidence in group members of their ability to accomplish meaningful tasks
- Instill a sense of responsibility in group members towards their group.
- Discuss the benefits of participation for the entire class

Procedural adjustments can always be made by the teacher, but the starting point is the plan. It is very difficult to adjust bedlam. Teachers who can clearly provide constructive learning expectations and lesson plans for students create structured learning environments that have clearly defined learning objectives and outcomes. Students need structure. Teachers should be organized in curriculum design, expectations and implementations.

Peer interactions that are not conducive to learning can impede the learning potential for the entire classroom. Disruptive students can hold classrooms hostage and typically do in classrooms with ineffective teacher facilitation of classroom management. A student who bullies another student in a classroom can impede the learning of not only that student, but also students who feel unsafe due to the lack of teacher intervention in dealing with the situation. However, if the student bully is confronted in a constructivist manner, the bully and the classroom learn about proactive conflict resolution and behavioral accountability. The bully becomes accountable for his/her behavior and understands that behavioral impact on his/her academic performance and that of the classroom learning access.

Classrooms that are designed to maximize learning potentials for all students are student centered and structured in a manner that is conducive to maximizing academic performance and social development. Teachers must have effective classroom management protocol in place to address student behavioral concerns and create orderly classrooms. Mutual student and teacher respect is a mainstay of proactive and constructivist classrooms.

Skill 3.6 Determines effective strategies for dealing with peer-related issues in given classroom situations.

Helping students to develop healthy self-images and self-worth are integral to the learning and development experiences. Learning is difficult when students are feeling bullied or negated in the school community. When a student is attending school from a homeless shelter or is lost in the middle of a parent's divorce or feeling a need to conform to fit into a certain student group, the student may be unable to effectively navigate the educational process or engage in the required academic expectations towards graduation or promotion to the next grade level or subject core level.

Most schools offer health classes that address teen issues around sexuality, self-image, peer pressure, nutrition, wellness, gang activity, drug engagement and a variety of other relevant teen experiences. Students are required to take a health class as a core class requirement and graduation requirement, so the incentive from the school's standpoint is that students are exposed to issues that directly affect them. However, one health class is not enough to effectively address the multiplicity of issues that could create a psychological or physiological trauma for a student.

Some schools have contracted with outside agencies to develop collaborative partnerships to bring in after school tutorial classes; gender and cultural specific groupings where students can deal authentically with integration of cultural and ethic experiences and lifestyles. Drug intervention programs and speakers on gang issues have created dynamic opportunities for school communities to bring the "untouchable" issues to the forefront and alleviate fears that are rampant in schools that are afraid to say "No to Drugs and Gangs." Both students and teachers must be taught about the world of teenagers and understand the social, psychological and learning implications that underscore the process of academic acquisition for society's most vulnerable citizens.

The complexity of peer related issues in high school learning communities escalates exponentially. First, in typical public high schools, there are more students in grade levels 9th-12th, who are interacting on a daily basis. The expectation of providing instructional practices for 32 students per class period and 160 students per day from a diversity of cultural, social, academic skill levels, and ethnic backgrounds can be daunting to a first year teacher. For the experienced teacher, each year brings adjustments in curriculum and student performance ability that may enhance or impede delivery of instruction.

Teachers are classroom negotiators who are constantly dealing with student peer related issues that occur in the classroom. Students are developmentally in a precarious stage of cognitive and social development as they struggle to meet the demands of a high school curriculum. For some students, it is difficult to make the transition between five different classes a day and this tension of transition is generally manifest in misbehavior in the classroom. Teachers who then become the mediators of student tensions must have a listing of accessible strategies to address and mediate student off-task behavioral concerns.

Student handbooks provide expectations for behavior and academic performance in classes. The stakes for students who are disruptive or who engage in serious offenses of disciplinary actions in the classrooms are much higher than a reprimand. Students can not only be suspended for serious offenses dealing with fights, drugs or constant disruptive conduct, but this suspension remains on their high school record and could impact college choices and acceptances. Both students and teachers are aware that the cost for peer related issues that escalate beyond the typical teacher strategy tool-kit could have far reaching implications beyond the classroom.

Skill 3.7   Understands how community characteristics (e.g., socioeconomic profile, opportunities for out-of-school educational experiences, availability of community resources) may affect students.

See Skill 3.3

COMPETENCY 4.0   UNDERSTANDS DIVERSE STUDENT POPULATIONS, AND USES THIS KNOWLEDGE TO DESCRIBE LEARNING OPPORTUNITIES AND ENVIRONMENTS THAT ADDRESS DIFFERENCES AMONG STUDENTS AND THAT PROMOTE APPRECIATION AND RESPECT FOR DIVERSITY.

Skill 4.1   Identifies strategies for working effectively with students from a variety of cultural backgrounds, students from various socioeconomic circumstances, students of both genders, students whose primary language is not English, students from a variety of geographical contexts (e.g., urban, rural, reservation, international), and students whose home situations involve a variety of family arrangements and lifestyles

A classroom is a community of learning, and when students learn to respect themselves and the members around them, learning is maximized. A positive environment, where open, discussion-oriented, non-threatening communication among all students can occur, is a critical factor in creating an effective learning culture. The teacher must take the lead and model appropriate actions and speech, and intervene quickly when a student makes a misstep and offends (often inadvertently) another.

Communication issues that the teacher in a diverse classroom should be aware of include:

- Be sensitive to terminology and language patterns that may exclude or demean students. Regularly switch between the use of "he" and "she" in speech and writing. Know and use the current terms that ethnic and cultural groups use to identify themselves (e.g., "Latinos" (favored) vs. "Hispanics").
- Be aware of body language that is intimidating or offensive to some cultures, such as direct eye contact, and adjust accordingly.
- Monitor your own reactions to students to ensure equal responses to males and females, as well as differently-performing students.
- Don't "protect" students from criticism because of their ethnicity or gender. Likewise, acknowledge and praise all meritorious work without singling out any one student. Both actions can make all students hyper-aware of ethnic and gender differences and cause anxiety or resentment throughout the class.
- Emphasize the importance of discussing and considering different viewpoints and opinions. Demonstrate and express value for all opinions and comments and lead students to do the same.

When teaching in diverse classrooms, teachers must also expect to be working and communicating with all kinds of students. The first obvious difference among students is gender. Interactions with male students are often different than those with female students. Depending on the lesson, female students are more likely to be interested in working with partners or perhaps even individually. On the other hand, male students may enjoy a more collaborative or hands-on activity. The gender of the teacher will also come into play when working with male and female students. Of course, every student is different and may not fit into a stereotypical role, and getting to know their students' preferences for learning will help teachers to truly enhance learning in the classroom.

Most class rosters will consist of students from a variety of cultures, as well. Teachers should get to know their students (of all cultures) so that they may incorporate elements of their cultures into classroom activities and planning. Also, getting to know about a student's background/cultural traditions helps to build a rapport with each student.

For students still learning English, teachers must make every attempt to communicate with that student daily. Whether it's with another student who speaks the same language, word cards, computer programs, drawings or other methods, teachers must find ways to encourage each student's participation. Of course, the teacher must also be sure the appropriate language services begin for the student in a timely manner, as well.

Teachers must also consider students from various socioeconomic backgrounds. These students are just as likely as anyone else to work well in a classroom; unfortunately, sometimes difficulties occur with these children when it comes to completing homework consistently. These students may need help deriving a homework system or perhaps need more attention on study or test-taking skills. Teachers should encourage these students as much as possible and offer positive reinforcements when they meet or exceed classroom expectations. Teachers should also watch these students carefully for signs of malnutrition, fatigue and possibly learning disorders.

Teachers should create a classroom climate that encourages extensive participation from the students. Collaborations and discussions are enhanced when students like and respect each other, and therefore, each student's learning can benefit. When everyone's thoughts and perspectives and ideas are offered, the class can consider each idea carefully in their discussion. The more students participate, the more learning is gained through a more thorough examination of the topic.

To create this environment, teachers must first model how to welcome and consider all points of view for the students. The teacher should then positively affirm and reinforce students for offering their ideas in front of the other students. Even if somewhat amiss, the teacher should receive the idea while perhaps offering a modification or corrected statement (for more factual pieces of information). The idea is for students to feel confident and safe in being able to express their thoughts or ideas. Only then will students be able to engage in independent discussions that consider and respect everyone's statements.

Students Acquiring English

There are many factors that impact someone's ability to pick up a second or third language. Age is one common factor. It is said that after a certain age (usually seven), learning a second language becomes dramatically harder. But there are also many social factors, such as anxiety, that influence language learning. Often, informal social settings are more conducive to second language learning. Motivation is another factor, obviously. A final important factor, particularly for teachers, is the strategies one uses to learn a language. For example, memorizing words out of context is not as effective as using words strategically for a real-life purpose.

Cognitive approaches to language learning focus on concepts. While words and grammar are important, when teachers use the cognitive approach, they focus on using language for conceptual purposes—rather than learning words and grammar for the sake of simply learning new words and grammatical structures. This approach focuses heavily on students' learning styles, and it cannot necessarily be pinned down as having specific techniques. Rather, it is more of a philosophy of instruction.

For more information, see www.everythingesl.net or http://www.nwrel.org/request/2003may/overview.html.

Skill 4.2 Demonstrates awareness of cultural differences (e.g., values, practices)

When diversity is promoted in learning environments and curriculum, both students and teachers are the beneficiaries of increased academic success. Using classrooms as vital resources for cultural and ethnic inclusion can assist students in contributing cultural norms and artifacts to the acquisition of learning. Teachers are able to create global thinkers by helping students identify cultural assumptions and biases that may direct the type of social and academic groupings that occur in the classroom and influence the type of thinking and construction of learning that happens within a classroom. For example, if a student is struggling in math, a teacher can examine the cultural aspect of learning math. For some students, math is insignificant when socioeconomic issues of poverty and survival are the daily reality of existence. When students see parents juggling finances, the only math that becomes important for them is that less is never enough to keep the lights on and mortgage paid.

When there is equity pedagogy, teachers can use a variety of instructional styles to facilitate diversity in cooperative learning and individualized instruction that will provide more opportunities for positive student experiences and academic success. Empowering the school culture and climate by establishing an anti-bias learning environment and promoting multicultural learning inclusion will discourage unfair labeling of certain students.

Teachers can use various toolkits of assessing integration and incorporation of ethnic and cultural inclusion in classroom. Effective promotion should translate into increased academic success and opportunities for all students. Looking at diverse or homogenous groupings in the classroom can provide teachers with opportunities to restructure cooperative learning groupings and increase diverse student interactions, which can provide increased improvements for school communities.

Using culture grams to help students understand different cultures is a useful tool for helping teachers profile student's learning styles and engagement in the classroom. Students can use technology to research how students in other cultures and in other states learn. The ability to communicate with other learners provides another way of compiling and categorizing cultural profiles that may assist teachers in identifying learning styles and how students acquire learning.

Skill 4.3   Demonstrates awareness of types of disabilities, developmental delays, and exceptionalities and of the implications for learning associated with these differences

The types of disabilities in children and adults are numerous. Some disabilities are entirely physical, while others are entirely related to learning and the mind. Some involve a combination of both. While it would be a disservice to say that all kids should display the same types of characteristics to be considered "normal," when abnormalities are noticed, such as a student's incredible ability to solve a math problem without working it out (a potential attribute of giftedness) or another student's extreme trouble with spelling (a potential attribute of dyslexia), a teacher may assume that a disability or exceptional ability is present.

Common learning disabilities include attention deficit hyperactivity disorder (where concentration can be very tough), auditory processing disorders (where listening comprehension is very difficult), visual processing disorders (where reading can be tough and visual memory may be impaired), dyslexia (where reading can be confusing), and many others. Physical disabilities include Down's Syndrome, where mental retardation may be a factor; cerebral palsy, where physical movement is impaired; and many others. Developmental disabilities might include the lack of ability to use fine motor skills.

When giftedness is observed, teachers should also concern themselves with ensuring that such children get the attention they need and deserve so that they can continue to learn and grow.

The list of possible disabilities goes on and on. When noticed, teachers might check with certain specialists at a school to determine if further testing or intervention is needed.

Skill 4.4   Identifies resources to address individuals' special needs

Individuals with Disabilities Act and Child Study Teams

Collaborative teams play a crucial role in meeting the needs of all students, and they are an important step to identifying students with special needs. Under the Individuals with Disabilities Act (IDEA), which federally mandates special education services in every state, it is the responsibility of public schools to ensure consultative, evaluative and if necessary, prescriptive services to children with special needs. In most school districts, this responsibility is handled by a collaborative group called the Child Study Team (CST). If a teacher or parent suspects a child to have academic, social or emotional problems, the child is referred to the CST.

This team, consisting of educational professionals (including teachers, specialists, the school psychologist, guidance, and other support staff) reviews the student's case and situation through meetings with the teacher and/or parents/guardians. The CST will determine what evaluations or tests are necessary, if any, and will also assess the results. Based on these results, the CST will suggest a plan of action if one is necessary.

One plan of action is an Academic Intervention Plan (AIP). An AIP consists of additional instructional services that are provided to the student in order to help them better achieve academically if the student has met certain criteria (such as scoring below the state reference point on standardized tests or performing more than two levels below grade-level).

Another plan of action is a 504 plan. A 504 plan is a legal document based on the provisions of the Rehabilitation Act of 1973 (which preceded IDEA). A 504 plan is a plan for instructional services to assist students with special needs in a regular education classroom setting. When a student's physical, emotional, or other impairments (such as Attention Deficit Disorder) impact his or her ability to learn in a regular education classroom setting, that student can be referred for a 504 meeting. Typically, the CST and perhaps even the student's physician or therapist will participate in the 504 meeting and review to determine if a 504 plan will be written.

Finally, a child referred to CST may qualify for an Individualized Education Plan (IEP). An IEP is a legal document which delineates the specific, adapted services a student with disabilities will receive. An IEP differs from a 504 plan in that the child must be identified for special education services to qualify for an IEP, and ALL students who receive special education services must have an IEP. Each IEP must contain statements pertaining to the student's present performance level, annual goals, related services and supplementary aids, testing modifications, a projected date of services, and assessment methods for monitoring progress. Each year, the CST and guardians must meet to review and update a student's IEP.

Inclusion, mainstreaming, and least restrictive environment

Inclusion, mainstreaming and least restrictive environment are interrelated policies under the IDEA, with varying degrees of statutory imperatives.

- Inclusion is the right of students with disabilities to be placed in the regular classroom.
- Lease restrictive environment is the mandate that children be educated to the maximum extent appropriate with their non-disabled peers.
- Mainstreaming is a policy where disabled students can be placed in the regular classroom, as long as such placement does not interfere with the student's educational plan

Skill 4.5   Describes strategies to ensure that all students participate to the greatest extent possible in classroom activities

The most important component in probing for student understanding is trust. Only if students trust their teacher will the communications process yield such things as the level of understanding a student has attained on any topic. If that component is in place, then creative questioning, which requires planning ahead, can sometimes reveal what the teacher needs to know. So can writing exercises that focus not on correctness but on a recording of the student's thoughts on a topic. Sometimes assuring the student that only the teacher will see what is written is helpful in freeing students to reveal their own thoughts. When a new unit is introduced, including vocabulary lessons related to the unit can help students find the words they need to talk or write about the topic.

Students can be taught the skills that lead to factual recall, and teaching those skills at very early grades will result in more successful students. For example, students need to know that experiencing a fact or an idea in several different ways increases the ability to recall it. Also, it will help them to know that experiences that involve more of the senses will increase the ability to recall the information.

See Skill 2.4

Skill 4.6   Demonstrates knowledge of strategies for promoting students' understanding and appreciation of diversity and for using diversity that exists within the classroom and the community to enhance all students' learning.

In personalized learning communities, relationships and connections between students, staff, parents and community members promote lifelong learning for all students. School communities that promote an inclusion of diversity in the classroom, community, curriculum and connections enable students to maximize their academic capabilities and educational opportunities. Setting school climates that are inclusive of the multicultural demographic student population create positive and proactive mission and vision themes that align student and staff expectations.

The following factors enable students and staff to emphasize and integrate diversity in student learning:

- Inclusion of multicultural themes in curriculum and assessments
- Creation of a learning environment that promotes multicultural research, learning, collaboration, and social construction of knowledge and application
- Providing learning tasks that emphasize student cognitive, critical thinking and problem-solving skills.
- Learning tasks that personalize the cultural aspects of diversity and celebrate diversity in the subject matter and student projects.
- Promotion of intercultural positive social peer interrelationships and connections.

Teachers communicate diversity in instructional practices and experiential learning activities that create curiosity in students who want to understand the interrelationship of cultural experiences. Students become self-directed in discovering the global world in and outside the classroom. Teachers understand that when diversity becomes an integral part of the classroom environment, students become global thinkers and doers.

In the intercultural communication model, students are able to learn how different cultures engage in both verbal and nonverbal modes of communicating meaning. Students who become multilingual in understanding the stereotypes that have defined other cultures are able to create new bonding experiences that will typify a more integrated global culture. Students who understand how to effectively communicate with diverse cultural groups are able to maximize their own learning experiences by being able to transmit, both verbally and non-verbally, cues and expectations in project collaborations and in performance based activities. The learning curve for teachers in intercultural understanding is exponential in that they are able to engage all learners in the academic process and learning engagement. Teaching students how to incorporate learning techniques from a cultural aspect enriches the cognitive expansion experience.

SUBAREA II. INSTRUCTIONAL PLANNING AND MANAGEMENT

COMPETENCY 5.0 UNDERSTANDS CURRICULUM DEVELOPMENT AND INSTRUCTIONAL PLANNING, AND APPLY THIS KNOWLEDGE TO DESCRIBE INSTRUCTION THAT PROMOTES ACHIEVEMENT OF ARIZONA ACADEMIC STANDARDS AND OTHER INSTRUCTIONAL GOALS.

Skill 5.1 Understands procedures used in classroom curricular decision-making (e.g., evaluating the current curriculum; defining scope and sequence; detecting gaps in the curriculum, modifying curriculum based on student characteristics, the structure of the subject matter, and relevance in meeting societal expectations).

Curriculum development today must consider many factors of alignment, scope, sequence, and design.

First, curriculum must be aligned to state standards, state and local assessments, and district and school goals. Curriculum alignment simply means that there is reflection in the curriculum to these elements. In other words, what students learn should reflect state standards. Usually, this also means that what students learn is tested on state assessments. When curriculum is aligned to district and school goals, it means that, for example, if the district wanted all students to learn how to live in a multi-cultural society, curriculum would address that theme in a variety of ways.

Second, scope is the "horizontal" aspect of curriculum. For example, if a topic of study in a biology class is invertebrate animals, the scope would define everything that must be taught for students to understand this concept. On the other hand, sequence is the outline of what should be taught before and after a particular subject. So, for example, a sequence in math might suggest that students should learn addition and subtraction before multiplication and division. Likewise, basic math topics, like those just described, should be taught prior to decimals and fractions. A sequence would line all that up.

Design considers the progression from the beginning of a unit of study to the end of a unit of study. First, curriculum should be designed with the end in mind. What do you want students to know and be able to do? And how would they prove that they know the material or have the skill? If that information has been defined, it is much easier to design a curriculum. Too often, curricula is designed only considering forward steps in a process without concern for what students should be getting out of the curriculum.

As a teacher implements a curriculum, the teacher should be familiar with three main things:

(a) The philosophy or principal aims of the curriculum—in other words, what the curriculum wants students to get out of it.
(b) The knowledge base of the curriculum. If teachers are not deeply familiar with what they are teaching to students, they will be very ineffective at getting students to learn it.
(c) The plan, scope, and sequence of the curriculum. What would students have learned prior? Where will they go next?

While all students need to have exposure to the same curriculum, not all students need to have the curriculum taught in the same way. **Differentiation** is the term used to describe the variations of curriculum and instruction that can be provided to an entire class of students.

There are three primary ways to differentiate:
- Content – The specifics of what is learned. This does not mean that whole units or concepts should be modified. However, within certain topics, specifics can be modified.
- Process – The route to learning the content. This means that not everyone has to learn the content in exactly the same method.
- Product – The result of the learning. Usually, a product is the end result or assessment of learning. For example, not all students are going to demonstrate complete learning on a quiz; likewise, not all students will demonstrate complete learning on a written paper.

There are two keys to successful differentiation:

- **Knowing what is essential in the curriculum.**
  Although certain things can be modified, other things must remain in-tact in a specific order. Disrupting central components of a curriculum can actually damage a student's ability to learn something successfully.
- **Knowing the needs of the students.**
  While this can take quite some time to figure out, it is very important that teachers pay attention to the interests, tendencies, and abilities of their students so that they understand how each of their students will best learn.

Many students will need certain concepts explained in greater depth; others may pick up on concepts rather quickly. For this reason, teachers will want to adapt curriculum in a way that allows students the opportunity to learn at their own pace, while also keeping the class as a community. While this can be difficult, the more creative a teacher is with the ways in which students can demonstrate mastery, the more fun the experience will be for students and teachers. Furthermore, teachers will reach students more successfully as they will tailor lesson plans, activities, groupings, and other elements of curriculum to each student's need.

Skill 5.2 Identifies strategies for developing interdisciplinary curricula (e.g., incorporating cross-disciplinary themes).

When the teacher actively and frequently models viewing from multiple perspectives as an approach to learning in the classroom, the students not only benefit through improved academic skill development, they also begin to adopt this approach for learning and contemplating as a personal skill. And the ability to consider a situation, issue, problem or event from multiple viewpoints is a skill that will serve the individual well, throughout his or her academic career and beyond.

Internalizing the concept of teaching from multiple perspectives starts by posing a simple challenge for oneself. You intend to introduce one fact or skill from your subject area to a student. You do so in the prescribed format—giving the standard explanation and ancillary examples of application. The student doesn't get it: doesn't acquire the skill and can't internalize the information. As the teacher, what do you do? Repeat the instruction, verbatim, until it sinks in? Chastise or cajole the student into acknowledging an understanding? Since you are genuinely concerned about the student's acquisition of skills and academic success, you will immediately realize that the dilemma is yours, not the student's, and you will seek different ways to communicate an understanding of the information so that the student will completely comprehend and acquire a meaningful skill. After all, if the student does not succeed, it is the teacher who has failed.

In determining a better approach for providing an understanding to the student, you would consider many options and define the more probable ones to be used for instruction. The process for identifying viable options would include answering the following questions:

- What different words or phrasing might be used to say the same thing?
- How would I explain an opposite condition or fact, and would a negative example provide an understanding through contrast?
- If I imagined that the problem/fact/skill which I want to teach were an object which I could move around in any direction, would I be able to notice distinctions from varying angles? Would I be able to identify the "object's" component parts? Could I revise my explanation to provide a better understanding by starting from a different component part, reordering the component parts or redefining the component parts?
- Is there something preexisting in the student's acquired knowledge/skills which I can use to redirect or reinforce my explanation by making reference or demonstrating a link?
- Is there something specific to the student's culture or life experience which could inform my explanation/instruction?

When planning instruction for a diverse group (or teaching about diversity, for that matter) incorporate teaching through the use of perspective. There is always more than one way to "see" or approach a problem, an example, a process, fact or event, or any learning situation. Varying approaches for instruction helps to maintain the students' interest in the material and enables the teacher to address the diverse needs of individuals to comprehend the material.

Curriculum objectives and instructional strategies may be inappropriate and unsuccessful when presented in a single format which relies on the student's understanding and acceptance of the values and common attributes of a specific culture which is not his or her own. Planning, devising and presenting material from a multicultural perspective can enable the teacher in a culturally diverse classroom to ensure that all the students achieve the stated, academic objective.

Even when the student population is largely culturally homogeneous, teaching with cultural perspective is always an asset to student comprehension and learning. History, as a subject, would be just one obvious example. The study of history includes the interactions of people from different cultures or subcultures. The point of view of, and impact on, each culture must be presented during instruction to ensure a comprehensive understanding of issues and events by the students. And in order to understand these points of view and impacts, it will be necessary to study the backgrounds of the cultures involved.

Interdisciplinary and thematic instruction, by definition and design, provide for teaching from perspective. Examples of effective, readily available instructional units are displayed, below.

Discovering Your World by Anita Yeoman

This integrated unit introduces students to various countries as they plan a trip around the world. The unit is very flexible and can be adapted for any middle-level grade and time period. It consists of detailed suggestions for planning a "journey" according to the needs of each class. Worksheets for planning an itinerary, making passports and calculating distances are included, together with peer and self evaluation sheets and tracking sheets. Students will utilize research skills as they learn about language, history, geography and culture of the countries they "visit" on their world trip.

Let's Create An Island by Philip Richards

In this unit students will create an island, following a set of suggestions, deciding on such things as its location, topography, climate, population, employment, form of government, leisure activities, education etc. It enables students to learn important geographic, scientific and civic concepts in a manner that is enjoyable and imaginative. For each activity a concept is taught as a class activity, followed by independent exercises to reinforce what has been taught. The students then this use this knowledge when creating their own island. Grades 6 – 9

Teaching from multiple perspectives opens the door to a world of ideas teachers can use to make education an interesting, fun and effective learning experience where every student can be included in the process and be successful in attaining the objectives. The possibilities may only be limited by the teacher's imagination. Should that limit actually be reached, the teacher has only to look to his or her colleagues to expand the horizon of teaching possibilities

A philosophy of teaching from perspective: It is less important which path we take, than that we all arrive at the same destination.

Skill 5.3   Evaluates curriculum materials and instructional resources (e.g., textbook, guest speaker, multi-media) for their appropriateness and relevance in presenting particular ideas or concepts.

In considering suitable learning materials for the classroom, the teacher must have a thorough understanding of the state-mandated competency-based curriculum. According to state requirements, certain objectives must be met in each subject taught at every designated level of instruction. It is necessary that the teacher become well acquainted with the curriculum for which he/she is assigned. The teacher must also be aware that it is unlawful to require students to study from textbooks or materials other than those approved by the state Department of Education.

Keeping in mind the state requirements concerning the objectives and materials, the teacher must determine the abilities of the incoming students assigned to his/her class or supervision. It is essential to be aware of their entry behavior—that is, their current level of achievement in the relevant areas. The next step is to take a broad overview of students who are expected to learn before they are passed on to the next grade or level of instruction. Finally, the teacher must design a course of study that will enable students to reach the necessary level of achievement, as displayed in their final assessments, or exit behaviors. Textbooks and learning materials must be chosen to fit into this context.

Once students' abilities are determined, the teacher will select the learning materials for the class. In choosing materials, teachers should also keep in mind that not only do students learn at different rates, but they bring a variety of cognitive styles to the learning process. Prior experiences influence the individual's cognitive style, or method of accepting, processing, and retaining information.

Most teachers chose to use textbooks, which are suitable to the age and developmental level of specific student populations. Textbooks reflect the values and assumptions of the society that produces them, while they also represent the knowledge and kills considered to be essential in becoming an educated adult. Finally, textbooks are useful to the school bureaucracy and the community, for they make public and accessible the private world of the classroom.

Aside from textbooks, there is a wide variety of materials available to today's teachers. Microcomputers are now commonplace, and some schools can now afford laser discs to bring alive the content of a reference book in text, motion, and sound. Hand-held calculators eliminate the need for drill and practice in number facts, while they also support a problem solving and process to mathematics. VCRs and DVD players are common and permit the use of home-produced or commercially produced movies. Textbook publishers often provide films, recordings, and software to accompany the text, as well as maps, graphics, and colorful posters to help students visualize what is being taught.

In addition, yesterday's libraries are today's media centers. Teachers can use multimedia projectors to project print, pictorial images and websites onto a screen for classroom viewing. Some teachers have chosen to replace chalkboards with interactive whiteboards (or Smartboards). These are large, touch-controlled screen that work with a projector and a computer. The projector throws the computer's desktop image onto the interactive whiteboard, which acts as both a monitor and an input device. Users can write on the interactive whiteboard in digital ink or use a finger to control computer applications by pointing, clicking and dragging, just as with a desktop mouse.

In an art or photography class, or any class in which it is helpful to display visual materials, slides can easily be projected onto a wall or a screen. Cameras are inexpensive enough to enable students to photograph and display their own work, as well as keep a record of their achievements in teacher files or student portfolios.

Skill 5.4   Describes procedures used in instructional planning (e.g., defining lesson or unit objectives, developing lesson plans).

Teaching was once seen as developing lesson plans, teaching, going home early and taking the summer off. However, the demands of a classroom involve much more than grading papers. To begin with, just writing lesson plans is very complicated. Lesson plans are important in guiding instruction in the classroom. Incorporating the nuts and bolts of a teaching unit, the lesson plan outlines the steps of teacher implementation and assessment of teacher instructional capacity and student learning capacity. Teachers are able to objectify and quantify learning goals and targets in terms of incorporating effective performance-based assessments and projected criteria for identifying when a student has learned the material presented.

All components of a lesson plan including the unit description, learning targets, learning experiences, explanation of learning rationale and assessments must be present to provide both quantifiable and qualitative data to ascertain whether student learning has taken place and whether effective teaching has occurred for the students. National and state learning standards must be taken into account because not only will the students be measured by the students' scores at the end of the year, the teacher and the school will also. So, not only must the teacher be knowledgeable about state and local standards, s/he must structure the class in ways that will meet those frameworks.

On the large scale, the teacher must think about the scope of the plans for the day, the week, the unit, the semester, the year. The teacher must decide on the subject matter for the unit, semester, year, making certain that it is appropriate to the age of the students, relevant to their real lives, and in their realm of anticipated interest. Should s/he introduce politically controversial issues or avoid them? These decisions must be made deliberatively on the basis of feedback from the students, at the same time keeping sight of the lesson objectives.

The teacher must be very knowledgeable about the writing of behavioral objectives that fall within the guidelines of the state and local expectations, and the objectives must be measurable so that when the unit or semester is complete, the teacher can know for sure whether the lesson goal was accomplished. Once long range goals have been identified and established, it is important to ensure that all goals and objectives are in aligned with student ability and needs. Some objectives may be too basic for a higher level student, while others cannot be met with a student's current level of knowledge. There are many forms of evaluating student needs to ensure that all goals set are challenging yet achievable.

Teachers should check a student's cumulative file for reading level and prior subject area achievement. This provides a basis for goal setting but shouldn't be the only method used. Depending on the subject area, basic skills test, reading level evaluations, writing samples, and/or interest surveys can all be useful in determining if all goals are appropriate. Informal observation should always be used as well. Finally, it is important to take into consideration the student's level of motivation when addressing student needs.

When given objectives by the school, county, or state, teachers may wish to adapt them so that they can meet the needs of their student population. For example, if a high level advanced class is given the objective, "*State five causes of World War II*," a teacher may wish to adapt the objective to a higher level. "*State five causes of World War II and explain how they contributed to the start of the war.*" Subsequently objectives can be modified for a lower level as well. "*From a list of causes, pick three that specifically caused World War II.*"

When organizing and sequencing objectives, remember that skills are building blocks. A taxonomy of educational objectives can be helpful to construct all organize objectives. Knowledge of material is low on a taxonomy and should be worked with early in the sequence. For example, memorizing definitions or memorizing famous quotes. Eventually, objectives should be developed to include higher level thinking such as comprehension (i.e., being able to use a definition); application (i.e., being able to apply the definition to other situations); synthesis (i.e., being able to add other information); and evaluation (i.e., being able to judge the value of something).

Emergent curriculum describes the projects and themes that classrooms embark on that have been inspired by the children's interests. The teacher uses all the tools of assessment available to know as much as possible about the students, and then continually assesses them over the period of the unit or semester. As the teacher gets to know them, s/he listens to what their interests are and creates a curriculum in response to what is learned from these observations.

Webbing is a recent concept related to the idea of emergent curriculum. The two main uses are planning and recording curriculum. Planning webs are used to generate ideas for activities and projects for the students from an observed interest such as rocks. Teachers work together to come up with ideas and activities for the children and to record them in a "web" format. Activities can be grouped by different areas of the room or by developmental domains. For example, clusters either fall under areas such as dramatic play or science areas or around domains such as language, cognitive, and physical development. Either configuration works; being consistent in each web is important. Any new activities that emerge throughout the unit can also be added to the web. The record will serve in the future to plan using activities that emerge from the children's play and ideas.

Skill 5.5 Recognizes key factors to consider in planning instruction (e.g., students' characteristics and prior experiences, available time and other resources, appropriate sequencing of lessons within units, instructional goals).

The first step in planning successful instruction is knowing what students will be held accountable for. While teachers may have the best of intentions in teaching numerous, exciting topics, there are only so many days in a school year. Furthermore, the more content is "covered" (skimmed over, so that students can be exposed to everything), the less students will have deep and lasting understandings of content. So, with that in mind, teachers will benefit from laying out all crucial standards throughout the year and aligning them in a fashion that allows for conceptual growth. Conceptual growth refers to concepts building upon one another. Certain topics simply should be taught before other topics.

Next, teachers should consider how students will be required to demonstrate proficiency of the various concepts. This is important, as all instruction should focus on making sure that students can indeed demonstrate proficiency.

Finally, as lessons and units are planned, to be most efficient with time, teachers should determine how much students already understand and how long it will take to fully teach the concepts. This will allow the teacher to develop lessons that build on students' background knowledge without repeating it. It will also help teachers manage teaching so many standards in a one year time period.

The concept of readiness is generally regarded as a developmentally based phenomenon. Various abilities, whether cognitive, affective, or psychomotor, are perceived to be dependent upon the mastery or development of certain prerequisite skills or abilities. Readiness, then, implies that there are necessary prior knowledge, experience, and readiness prerequisites. Students should not engage in the new task until first acquiring the necessary readiness foundation.

It should be noted, then, that a concept such as "readiness to learn" is too broad to be meaningful. Readiness needs to be considered in terms of readiness to "learn science" or, even more accurately, readiness to "learn photosynthesis." Since it is not feasible for the classroom teacher to assess each student's readiness for each lesson, mastery of one lesson is generally assumed to imply readiness for the next sequential lesson.

However, at each grade level, there exist readiness expectations and assumptions based on the previous year's instruction. Students who have not yet mastered those concepts are not ready to progress. Failure on the part of the teacher to address student deficiencies may lead to failure of the student to learn the new material.

Readiness for subject area learning is dependent not only on prior knowledge, but also on affective factors such as interest, motivation, and attitude. These factors are often more influential on student learning than the pre-existing cognitive base.

Skill 5.6   Analyzes a given lesson or unit plan in terms of organization, completeness, feasibility, etc.

Lesson plans are important in guiding instruction in the classroom. Incorporating the nuts and bolts of a teaching unit, the lesson plan outlines the steps of teacher implementation and assessment of teacher instructional capacity and student learning capacity. Teachers are able to objectify and quantify learning goals and targets in terms of incorporating effective performance-based assessments and projected criteria for identifying when a student has learned the material presented. All components of a lesson plan including the unit description, learning targets, learning experiences, explanation of learning rationale and assessments must be present to provide both quantifiable and qualitative data to ascertain whether student learning has taken place and whether effective teaching has occurred for the students. A typical format would include the following items below:

1. Written instructional lesson plan – These are guidelines for what is being taught and how the students will be able to access the information. Subsequent evaluations and assessments will determine whether students have learned or correctly processed the subject content being taught.

2. Unit Description – This provides a description of the learning and classroom environment.
   a. Classroom Characteristics - Describes the physical arrangements of the classroom, along with the student grouping patterns for the lesson being taught. Classroom rules and consequences should be clearly posted and visible.
   b. Student Characteristics – Describes the demographics of the classroom including student number, gender, cultural and ethnic backgrounds, along with Special Education students with IEPs (Individualized Education Plans).

3. Learning Goals/Targets/Objectives – This defines the expectations of the lessons. Are the learning goals appropriate to the state learning standards and district academic goals? Are the targets appropriate for the grade level, subject content area and inclusive of a multicultural perspective and global viewpoint.

4. Learning Experiences for students - How will student learning be supported using the learning goals?

   a. What prior knowledge or experiences will the students bring to the lesson? How will you check and verify that student knowledge?

   b. How will you engage all students in the classroom? How will students who have been identified as marginalized in the classroom be engaged in the lesson unit?

   c. How will the lesson plan be modified for students with IEPs and how will Special Education students be evaluated for learning and processing of the modified lesson targets?

   d. How will the multicultural aspect be incorporated into the lesson plan?

   e. What interdisciplinary links and connections will be used to incorporate across other subject areas?

   f. What types of assessments/evaluations will be used to test student understanding and processing of the lesson plan?

   g. How will students be cooperatively grouped to engage in the lesson?

   h. What internet links are provided in the lesson plan?

5. Rationales for Learning Experiences – This will provide data on how the lesson plan addresses student learning goals and objectives, including whether the lesson provides accommodations for students with IEPs and provides support for marginalized students in the classroom.

6. Assessments - Pre- and post- assessments will be written that evaluate student learning as it correlates to the learning goals and objectives. Do the assessments address the cultural needs and inclusion of students?

Skill 5.7   Describes strategies for collaborating with others to plan and implement interdisciplinary instruction.

According to Walther-Thomas et al (2000), "Collaboration for Inclusive Education," ongoing professional development that provides teachers with opportunities to create effective instructional practice is vital and necessary. A comprehensive approach to professional development is perhaps the most critical dimension of sustained support for successful program implementation." The inclusive approach incorporates learning programs that include all stakeholders in defining and developing high quality programs for students. Figure 1 below shows how an integrated approach of stakeholders can provide the optimal learning opportunity for all students.

Figure 1-Integrated Approach to Learning

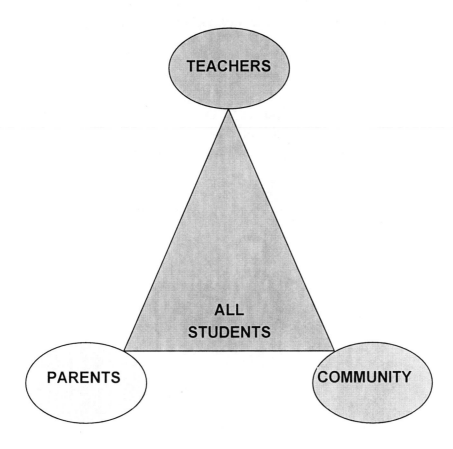

In the integrated approach to learning, teachers, parents, and community support become the integral apexes to student learning. The focus and central core of the school community is triangular as a representation of how effective collaboration can work in creating success for student learners. The goal of student learning and achievement now become the heart of the school community. The direction of teacher professional development in constructing effective instruction is clearly articulated in a greater understanding of facilitating learning strategies that develop skills and education equity for students.

Teachers need diversity in their instructional toolkits, which can provide students with clear instruction, mentoring, inquiry, challenge, performance-based assessment, and journal reflections on their learning processes. For teachers, having a collaborative approach to instruction fosters for students a deeper appreciation of learning, subject matter and knowledge acquisition. Implementing a consistent approach to learning from all stakeholders will create equitable educational opportunities for all learners.

Research has shown that educators who collaborate become more diversified and effective in implementation of curriculum and assessment of effective instructional practices. The ability to gain additional insight into how students learn and modalities of differing learning styles can increase a teacher's capacity to develop proactive instruction methods. Teachers who team-teach or have daily networking opportunities can create a portfolio of curriculum articulation and inclusion for students.

People in business are always encouraged to network in order to further their careers. The same can be said for teaching. If English teachers get together and discuss what is going on in their classrooms, those discussions make the whole much stronger than the parts. Even if there are not formal opportunities for such networking, it's wise for schools or even individual teachers to develop them and seek them out.

COMPETENCY 6.0   **UNDERSTANDS HOW TO USE FORMAL AND INFORMAL ASSESSMENT TO LEARN ABOUT STUDENTS, PLAN INSTRUCTION, MONITOR STUDENT UNDERSTANDING, AND MODIFY INSTRUCTION TO ENHANCE STUDENT LEARNING AND DEVELOPMENT.**

Skill 6.1   **Demonstrates knowledge of the characteristics, uses, advantages, and limitations of different types of informal and formal assessments (e.g., portfolio, teacher-designed classroom test, embedded assessment, performance assessment, peer assessment, student self-assessment, teacher observation, standardized achievement test.**

Types of Assessment

It is useful to consider the types of assessment procedures that are available to the classroom teacher. The types of assessment discussed below represent many of the more common types, but the list is not comprehensive.

Anecdotal records

These are notes recorded by the teacher concerning an area of interest or concern with a particular student. These records should focus on observable behaviors and should be descriptive in nature. They should not include assumptions or speculations regarding effective areas such as motivation or interest. These records are usually compiled over a period of several days to several weeks.

Rating scales & checklists

These assessments are generally self-appraisal instruments completed by the students or observations-based instruments completed by the teacher. The focus of these is frequently on behavior or affective areas such as interest and motivation.

Portfolio assessment

The use of student portfolios for some aspect of assessment has become quite common. The purpose, nature, and policies of portfolio assessment vary greatly from one setting to another. In general, though, a student's portfolio contains samples of work collected over an extended period of time. The nature of the subject, age of the student, and scope of the portfolio, all contribute to the specific mechanics of analyzing, synthesizing, and otherwise evaluating the portfolio contents.

In most cases, the student and teacher make joint decisions as to which work samples go into the student's portfolios. A collection of work compiled over an extended time period allows teacher, student, and parents to view the student's progress from a unique perspective. Qualitative changes over time can be readily apparent from work samples. Such changes are difficult to establish with strictly quantitative records typical of the scores recorded in the teacher's grade book.

Questioning

One of the most frequently occurring forms of assessment in the classroom is oral questioning by the teacher. As the teacher questions the students, she collects a great deal of information about the degree of student learning and potential sources of confusing for the students. While questioning is often viewed as a component of instructional methodology, it is also a powerful assessment tool.

Tests

Tests and similar direct assessment methods represent the most easily identified types of assessment. Thorndike (1997) identifies three types of assessment instruments:

1. Standardized achievement tests
2. Assessment material packaged with curricular materials
3. Teacher-made assessment instruments
   - Pencil and paper test
   - Oral tests
   - Product evaluations
   - Performance tests
   - Effective measures (p.199)

Kellough and Roberts (1991) take a slightly different perspective. They describe "three avenues for assessing student achievement:
   a) what the learner says
   b) what the learner does, and
   c) what the learner writes..." (p.343)

Types of tests

Formal tests are those tests that have been standardized on a large sample population. The process of standardization provides various comparative norms and scales for the assessment instrument. The term "informal test" includes all other tests. Most publisher-provided tests and teacher-made tests are informal tests by this definition. Note clearly that an "informal" test is not necessarily unimportant. A teacher-made final exam, for example, is informal by definition because it has not been standardized.

Skill 6.2 **Uses measurement principles and assessment concepts (e.g., validity, reliability, bias) to determine the appropriateness of a formal or informal assessment instrument in a given situation.**

Purposes for Assessment

There are several different classification systems used to identify the various purposes for assessment. A compilation of several lists identifies some common purposes such as the following:

1. Diagnostic assessments are used to determine individual weakness and strengths in specific areas.
2. Readiness assessments measure prerequisite knowledge and skills.
3. Interest and attitude assessments attempt to identify topics of high interest or areas in which students may need extra motivational activities.
4. Evaluation assessments are generally program or teacher focused.
5. Placement assessments are used for purposes of grouping students or determining appropriate beginning levels in leveled materials.
6. Formative assessments provide on-going feedback on student progress and the success of instructional methods and materials.
7. Summative assessments define student accomplishment with the intent to determine the degree of student mastery or learning that has taken place.

For most teachers, assessment purposes vary according to the situation. It may be helpful to consult several sources to help formulate an overall assessment plan. Kellough and Roberts (1991) identify six purposes for assessment. These are:

1. To evaluate and improve student learning
2. To identify student strengths and weaknesses
3. To assess the effectiveness of a particular instructional strategy
4. To evaluate and improve program effectiveness
5. To evaluate and improve teacher effectiveness
6. To communicate to parents their children's progress (p.341)

Validity and Reliability

A desirable assessment is both reliable and valid. Without adequate reliability and validity, an assessment provides unusable results. A reliable assessment provides accurate and consistent results; there is little error from one time to the next. A valid assessment is one which tests what it intends to test.

Reliability is directly related to correlation. A perfect positive correlation equals + 1.00 and a perfect negative correlation equals -1.00. The reliability of an assessment tool is generally expressed as a decimal to two places (eg. 0.85). This decimal number describes the correlation that would be expected between two scores if the same student took the test two times.

Actually, there are several ways to estimate the reliability of an instrument. The method which is conceptually the most clear is the test-retested method. When the same test is administered again to the same students, if the test is perfectly reliable, each student will receive the same score each time. Even as the scores of individual students vary some from one time to the next, it is desirable for the rank order of the students to remain unchanged. Other methods of estimating reliability operate off of the same conceptual framework. Split-half methods divide a single test into two parts and compare them. Equivalent forms methods use two versions of the same test and compare test. With some types of assessment, such as essays and observation reports, reliability concerns also deal with the procedures and criteria used for scoring. The inter-rater reliability asks the question: How much will the results vary depending on who is scoring or rating the assessment data?

There are three commonly described types of validity: content validity, criterion validity, and construct validity. Content validity describes the degree to which a test actually tests, say, arithmetic. Story problems on an arithmetic test will lower is validity as a measure of arithmetic since reading ability will also be reflected in the results. However, note that it remains a valid test of the ability to solve story problems. Criterion validity is so named because of the concern with the test's ability to predict performance on another measure or test. For example, a college admissions test is highly valid if it predicts very accurately those students who will attain high GPAs at that college. The criterion in this case is college GPA. Construct validity is concerned with describing the usefulness or reality of what is being tested. The recent interest in multiple intelligences, instead of a single IQ score, is an example of the older construct of intelligence being reexamined as potentially several distinct constructs.

A student's readiness for a specific subject is not an absolute concept, but is determined by the relationship between the subject matter or topic and the student's prior knowledge, interest, motivation, attitude, experience and other similar factors.

Thus, the student's readiness to learn about the water cycle depends on whether the student already knows related concepts such as evaporation, condensation, and filtration. Readiness, then, implies that there is not a "gap" between what the student knows and the prerequisite knowledge base for learning.

A pretest designed to assess significant and related prerequisite skill and abilities is the most common method of identifying the student's readiness. This assessment should focus, not on the content to be introduced, but on prior knowledge judged to be necessary for understanding the new content. A pretest, which focuses on the new content, may identify students who do not need the new instruction (who have already mastered the material), but it will not identify students with readiness gaps.

The most common areas of readiness concerns fall in the basic academic skill areas. Mastery of the basic skill areas is a prerequisite for almost all subject area learning. Arithmetic skills and some higher level mathematics skills are generally necessary for science learning or for understanding history and related time concepts. Reading skills are necessary throughout the school years and beyond. A student with poor reading skills is at a disadvantage when asked to read a textbook chapter independently. Writing skills, especially handwriting, spelling, punctuation, and mechanics, are directly related to success in any writing-based activity. A weakness in any of these basic skill areas may at first glance appear to be a difficulty in understanding the subject area. A teacher who attempts to help the student master the subject matter through additional emphasis on the content will be misusing instructional time and frustrating the student. An awareness of readiness issues helps the teacher to focus on treating the underlying deficiency instead of focusing on the overt symptoms.

Once a readiness gap has been identified, then the teacher can provide activities designed to close the gap. Specific activities may be of almost any form. Since most learning builds upon previous learning, there are few activities or segments of learning that can be viewed solely as readiness or non-readiness activities.

While growth and maturation rates vary greatly from individual to individual, there are some generalizations that can be made concerning developmental characteristics of children. Most children appear to go through identifiable, sequential stages of growth and maturation, although not at the same rate. For the curriculum developers, it is often necessary to make some generalizations about the development level of the students of a particular age group or grade level. These generalizations, then, provide a framework for establishing the expectations of the children's performance. Textbooks, scope and sequence charts, school curriculum planners, and more, translate these generalizations into plans and expectations for the students. The curriculum plan that emerges identifies general goals and expectations for the average student.

One of the teacher's responsibilities in this situation is to realize the nature of the initial rough estimate of what is appropriate for a given group of students. The teacher should expect to modify and adjust the instructional program based on the needs and abilities of the students. A teacher may do this by grouping students for alternative instruction, adjusting or varying the materials (textbooks), varying the teaching methods, or varying the learning tasks.

Skill 6.3   Interprets assessment results

Subjective tests put the student in the driver's seat. These types of assessments usually consist of short answer, longer essays or problem solving that involves critical thinking skills requiring definitive proof from the short reading passages to support your answer. Sometimes teachers provide rubrics that include assessment criteria for high scoring answers and projects. Sometimes, the rubric is as simple as a checklist, and other times, a maximum point value is awarded for each item on the rubric. Either way, rubrics provide a guideline of the teacher's expectations for the specifics of the assignment. The teacher usually discusses and/or models what is expected to fulfill each guideline, as well as provides a detailed outline of these expectations for reference.

For example, students being asked to write a research paper might be provided with a rubric. An elementary teacher may assign a total of 50 points for the entire paper. The rubric may award ten points for note taking quality, ten points for research skills, twenty points for content covered, five points for creative elements, and five points for organization and presentation. Then a certain number of points will be awarded in accordance with the students' performance. Rubrics allow students to score in multiple areas, rather than simply on a final product.

Another assessment measure that teachers should be able to interpret is the Lexile reading score. As the most widely adopted reading measure in use today, Lexiles give educators the confidence to choose materials that will improve student reading skills across the curriculum and at home. Tens of thousands of books and tens of millions of articles have Lexile measures, hundreds of publishers Lexile their materials and all major standardized tests can report student reading scores in Lexiles.

The Lexile Framework for Reading is a scientific approach to reading measurement that matches readers to text. The Lexile Framework measures both reader ability and text difficulty on the same scale, called the Lexile scale. This approach allows educators to manage reading comprehension and encourage reader progress using Lexile measures and a broad range of Lexile products, tools and services.

For more information on Lexile scores, visit http://www.lexile.com/

Skill 6.4   Describes adjustments to lessons and activities based on assessment results

There are many ways to evaluate a child's knowledge and assess his/her learning needs. In recent years, the emphasis has shifted from "mastery testing" of isolated skills to authentic assessments of what children know. Authentic assessments allow the teacher to know more precisely what each individual student knows, can do, and needs to do. Authentic assessments can work for both the student and the teacher in becoming more responsible for learning.

One of the simplest most efficient ways for the teacher to get to know his/her students is to conduct an entry survey. This is a record that provides useful background information about the students as they enter a class or school. Collecting information through an entry survey will give valuable insights into a student's background knowledge and experience. Teachers can customize entry surveys according to the type of information considered valuable. Some of the information that may be incorporated include student's name and age, family members, health factors, special interests, strengths, needs, fears, etc., parent expectations, languages spoken in the home, what the child likes about school, etc.

At the beginning of each school term the teacher will likely feel compelled to conduct some informal evaluations in order to obtain a general awareness of his/her students. These informal evaluations should be the result of a learning activity rather than a "test" and may include classroom observations, collections of reading and writing samples, and notations about the students' cognitive abilities as demonstrated by classroom discussions and participation including the students' command of language. The value of these informal evaluations cannot be underestimated. These evaluations, if utilized effectively, will drive instruction and facilitate learning.

After initial informal evaluations have been conducted and appropriate instruction follows, teachers will need to fine tune individual evaluations in order to provide optimum learning experiences. Some of the same types of evaluations can be used on an ongoing basis to determine individual learning needs as were used to determine initial general learning needs. It is somewhat more difficult to choose an appropriate evaluation instrument for elementary-aged students than for older students. Therefore, teachers must be mindful of developmentally appropriate instruments. At the same time, teachers must be cognizant of the information that they wish to attain from a specific evaluation instrument. Ultimately, these two factors—students' developmental stage and the information to be derived—will determine which type of evaluation will be most appropriate and valuable. There are few commercially designed assessment tools that will prove to be as effective as the tool that is constructed by the teacher.

A simple-to-administer, information-rich evaluation of a child's reading strengths and weaknesses is the running reading record. "This technique for recording reading behavior is the most insightful, informative, and instructionally useful assessment procedure you can use for monitoring a child's progress in learning to read;" (Traill, 1993) The teacher uses a simple coding system to record what a child does while reading text out loud. At a later time the teacher can go back to the record and assess what the child knows about reading and what the teacher needs to address in an effort to help the student become a better reader.

If the teacher is evaluating a child's writing, it is a good idea to discourage the child from erasing his/her errors and to train the child to cross out errors with a single line so that the teacher can actually see the process that the student went through to complete a writing assignment. This writing becomes an important means of getting to know about students' writing and is an effective, valuable writing evaluation.

Mathematics skills can be evaluated informally by observing students as they work at their seats or perform at the board. Teachers can see if the students know basic computation skills, if they understand place value, or if they transpose numbers simply by watching them as they solve computation problems. Some teachers may prefer to administer some basic computation "tests" to determine a student's mathematics strengths and weaknesses. Although these "tests" are not as effective or thorough in assessing students, they are quick and easy to administer.

One of the most valuable and effective assessment tools available to any teacher is the classroom observation. As instructional decision makers, teachers must base their instructional strategies upon students' needs. An astute observer of student behaviors and performance is most capable of choosing instructional strategies that will best meet the needs of the learners. Classroom observations take place within the context of the learning environment thus allowing the observer the opportunity to notice natural behaviors and performances.

Classroom observations should be sensitive and systematic in order to permit a constant awareness of student progress. One of the shortcomings of classroom observations is that they are often performed randomly and frequently are focused on those students whose behaviors are less than desirable. If the teacher establishes a focused observation process then observations become more valuable. It has been suggested that a teacher focus his/her observations on five or six students at a time for a period of one to two weeks.

In order for observations to truly be useful, teachers must record the information obtained from observations. When doing a formal behavioral observation, the teacher will write what the child is doing for a designated time period. At times the teacher will tally the occurrences of specific behaviors within a designated time period. When making focused observations that are ongoing, the teacher may simply use a blank piece of paper with only the student's name and date written on it and space for the teacher to write anecdotal notes. Other teachers might write on post-it notes and put the information in a student's file. If it is not possible to record the information as it occurs and is observed, it is critical that it be recorded as soon as possible in order to maintain accuracy.

Sometimes it is helpful to do an observation simply to watch for frequency of a specific behavior. An observation can answer questions such as: Is the student on-task during independent work time? Is the student interacting appropriately with peers? Is the student using materials appropriately? These behaviors can be tallied on a piece of paper with the student's name and date of observation.

Classroom observations can provide the teacher with one of the most comprehensive means of knowing their students. Teachers can observe students to see how they interact with their peers, to see which activities they choose, what they like to read, and how frequently they choose to work alone. "Everything you hear a child say and see a child do is a glimpse into a mind and a source of information to 'know' from." (Traill, 1993)

Skill 6.5   Communicates assessment results

Research proves that the more families are involved in a child's educational experience, the more that child will succeed academically. The problem is that often teachers assume that involvement in education simply means that the parents show up to help at school events or participate in parental activities on campus. With this belief, many teachers devise clever strategies to increase parental involvement at school. However, just because a parent shows up to school and assists with an activity does not mean that the child will learn more. Many parents work all day long and cannot assist in the school. Teachers, therefore, have to think of different ways to encourage parental and family involvement in the educational process.

Quite often, teachers have great success with involving families by just informing families of what is going on in the classroom. Newsletters are particularly effective at this. Parents love to know what is going on in the classroom, and this way, they'll feel included. In newsletters, for example, teachers can provide suggestions on how parents can help with the educational goals of the school. For example, teachers can recommend that parents read with their children for twenty minutes per day. To add effectiveness to that, teachers can also provide suggestions on what to do when their children come across difficult words or when they ask a question about comprehension. This gives parents practical strategies.

Parents often equate phone calls from teachers with news about misbehaviors of their children. Teachers can change that tone by calling parents with good news. Or they can send positive notes home with students. By doing this, when negative phone calls need to be made, teachers will have greater success.

Teachers can also provide very specific suggestions to individual parents. For example, let's say a student needs additional assistance in a particular subject. The teacher can provide tips to parents to encourage and increase deeper understandings in the subject outside of class.

When you find it necessary to communicate (whether by phone, letter, or in person) with a parent regarding a concern about a student, allow yourself a "cooling off" period before making contact with the parent. It is important that you remain professional and objective. Your purpose for contacting the parent is to elicit support and additional information that may have a bearing on the student's behavior or performance. Be careful that you do not demean the child and do not appear antagonistic or confrontational. Be aware that the parent is likely to be quite uncomfortable with the bad news and will respond best if you take a cooperative, problem solving approach to the issue. It is also a nice courtesy to notify parents of positive occurrences with their children. The teacher's communication with parents should not be limited to negative items.

Communicating with Students

How can a teacher provide good feedback so that students will learn from their assessments? First, language should be helpful and constructive. Critical comments do not necessarily help students learn. They may become defensive or hurt, and therefore, they may be more focused on the perceptions than the content. Language that is constructive and helpful will guide students to specific actions and recommendations that would help them improve in the future.

When teachers provide timely feedback, they increase the chance that students will reflect on their thought-processes as they originally produced the work. When feedback comes weeks after the production of an assignment, the student may not remember what it is that caused him or her to respond in a particular way.

Specific feedback is particularly important. Comments like, "This should be clearer" and "Your grammar needs to be worked on" provide information that students may already know. They may already know they have a problem with clarity. What they can benefit from is commentary that provides very specific actions students could take to make something more clear or to improve his or her grammar.

When teachers provide feedback on a set of assignments, for example, they enhance their students' learning by teaching students how to use the feedback. For example, returning a set of papers can actually do more than provide feedback to students on their initial performance. Teachers can ask students to do additional things to work with their original products, or they can even ask students to take small sections and re-write based on the feedback. While written feedback will enhance student learning, having students do something with the feedback encourages even deeper learning and reflection.

Experienced teachers may be reading this and thinking, "When will I ever get the time to provide so much feedback?" Although detailed and timely feedback is important—and necessary—teachers do not have to provide it all the time to increase student learning. They can also teach students how to use scoring guides and rubrics to evaluate their own work, particularly before they turn it in. One particularly effective way of doing this is by having students examine models and samples of proficient work. Over years, teachers should collect samples, remove names and other identifying factors, and show these to students so that they understand what is expected of them. Often, when teachers do this, they will be surprised to see how much students gain from this in terms of their ability to assess their own performance.

Finally, teachers can help students develop plans for revising and improving upon their work, even if it is not evaluated by the teacher in the preliminary stages. For example, teachers can have students keep track of words they commonly misspell, or they can have students make personal lists of areas they feel on which they need to focus.

Communicating with Parents/Guardians

The major questions for parents in understanding student performance criterion-referenced data assessment are, "Are students learning?" and "How well are students learning?" Providing parents with a collection of student learning assessment data related to student achievement and performance is a quantifiable response to the questions. The National Study of School Evaluation (NSSE) 1997 research on School Improvement: Focusing on Student performance adds the following additional questions for parent focus on student learning outcomes:

- What are the types of assessments of student learning that are used in the school?
- What do the results of the data assessments indicate about the current levels of student learning performance? About future predictions? What were the learning objectives and goals?
- What are the strengths and limitations in student learning and achievement?
- How prepared are students for further education or promotion to the next level of education?
- What are the trends seen in student learning in various subject areas or overall academic learning?

Providing parents with opportunities to attend workshops on data discussions with teachers and administrators creates additional opportunity for parents to ask questions and become actively involved in monitoring their student's educational progress. With state assessments, parents should look for the words "passed" or "met/exceeded standards" in interpreting the numerical data on student reports. Parents who maintain an active involvement in their students' education will attend school opportunities to promote their understanding of academic and educational achievement for students.

See also Skill 11.4

COMPETENCY 7.0   **UNDERSTAND PRINCIPLES AND TECHNIQUES ASSOCIATED WITH VARIOUS INSTRUCTIONAL STRATEGIES AND APPROACHES, AND USES THIS KNOWLEDGE TO PROMOTE ACHIEVEMENT OF ARIZONA ACADEMIC STANDARDS AND OTHER INSTRUCTIONAL GOALS.**

Skill 7.1   **Identifies the uses, benefits, and limitations of a specific instructional approach (e.g., direct instruction, cooperative learning, inquiry-based learning, interdisciplinary instruction, whole-group and small-group discussion, lecture, hands-on activity, peer tutoring, technology-based instruction, individualized instruction) in relation to given purposes or students (including those with special needs).**

Direct Instruction

Siegfried Engelmann and Dr. Wesley Becker, and several other researchers proposed what they call direct instruction, a teaching method that emphasizes well-developed and carefully-planned lessons with small learning increments. It assumes that clear instruction that eliminates misinterpretations will improve outcomes. Their approach is being used by thousands of schools. It recommends that the popular valuing of teacher creativity and autonomy be replaced by a willingness to follow certain carefully prescribed instructional practices. At the same time, it encourages the retention of hard work, dedication, and commitment to students. It demands that teachers adopt and internalize the belief that all students, if properly taught, can learn.

Discovery Learning

Beginning at birth, discovery learning is a normal part of the growing-up experience, and this naturally occurring phenomenon can be used to improve the outcomes in your classrooms. Discovery learning in the classroom is based upon inquiry. It has been a factor in all the advances mankind has made through the years. For example, Rousseau constantly questioned his world, particularly the philosophies and theories that were commonly accepted. Dewey, himself a great discoverer, wrote, "There is an intimate and necessary relation between the processes of actual experience and education." Piaget, Bruner, and Papert have all recommended this teaching method. In discovery learning, students solve problems by using their own experience and prior knowledge to determine what truths can be learned. Bruner wrote "Emphasis on discovery in learning has precisely the effect on the learner of leading him to a constructionist, to organize what he is encountering in a manner not only designed to discover regularity and relatedness, but also to avoid the kind of information drift that fails to keep account of the uses to which information might have to be put."

Whole Group Discussion

Whole group discussion can be used in a variety of settings, but the most common is in the discussion of an assignment. Since learning is peer-based with this strategy, students gain a different perspective on the topic, as well as learn to respect the ideas of others. One obstacle that can occur with this teaching method is that the same people tend to participate over and over and the same people do not participate time after time. However, with proper teacher guidance during this activity, whole group discussions are highly valuable.

Case Method Learning

Providing an opportunity for students to apply what they learn in the classroom to real-life experiences has proven to be an effective way of both disseminating and integrating knowledge. The case method is an instructional strategy that engages students in active discussion about issues and problems inherent in practical application. It can highlight fundamental dilemmas or critical issues and provide a format for role playing ambiguous or controversial scenarios. Obviously, a successful class discussion involves planning on the part of the instructor and preparation on the part of the students. Instructors should communicate this commitment to the students on the first day of class by clearly articulating course expectations. Just as the instructor carefully plans the learning experience, the students must comprehend the assigned reading and show up for class on time, ready to learn.

Concept Mapping

Concept mapping is a common tool used by teachers in various disciplines, and there are many kinds of maps that have been developed for this purpose. They are useful devices, but each teacher must determine which is appropriate for use in his/her own classroom. Following is a common map that is used in writing courses:

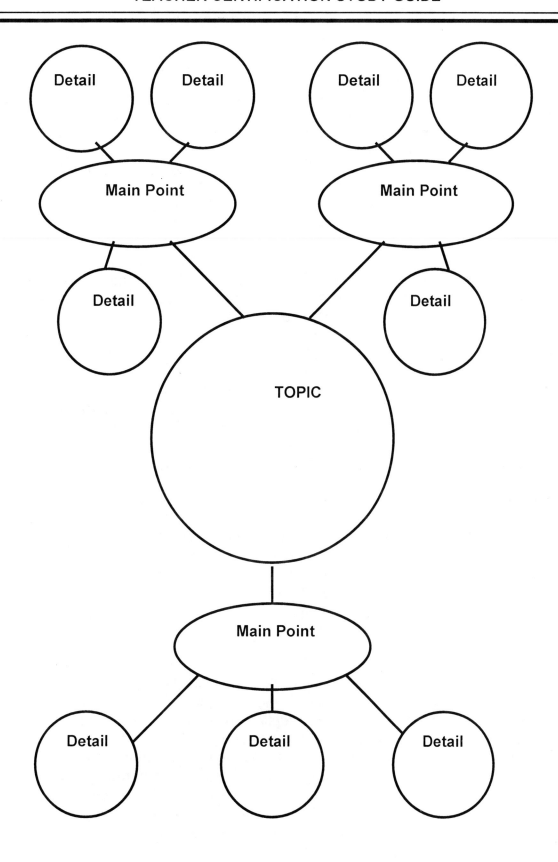

Inquiry

All learning begins with the learner. What children know and what they want to learn are not just constraints on what can be taught; they are the very foundation for learning. Dewey's description of the four primary interests of the child are still appropriate starting points:
1. the child's instinctive desire to find things out
2. in conversation, the propensity children have to communicate
3. in construction, their delight in making things
4. in their gifts of artistic expression.

Questioning

Questioning is a teaching strategy as old as Socrates. The important thing for the teacher to remember is that it must be deliberative and carefully planned. This is an important tool for leading students into critical thinking.

Play

There are so many useful games available that the most difficult task is choosing which will fit into your classroom. Some are electronic, some are board games, and some are designed to be played by a child individually. Even in those cases, a review of the results by the entire classroom can be a useful learning experience.

Learning centers

In a flexible classroom where students have some time when they can choose which activity they will participate in, learning centers are extremely important. Teachers must use out-of-class time to create them, collect the items that will make them up, and then set them up. In some classes, the students might participate in creating a learning center.

Small group work

In the diverse classrooms, small group work is vital. Children can be grouped according to their level of development or the small groups themselves can be diverse, giving the students who are struggling an opportunity to learn from a student who is already proficient. The better prepared student will learn from becoming a source for the weaker student, and the weaker student may be more likely to accept help from another student sometimes than from the teacher.

Revisiting

Revisiting should occur during a unit, at the end of a unit, and at the end of a semester. In other words, giving students more than one opportunity to grasp principles and skills and to integrate them is practical teaching theory.

Reflection

Teaching can move along so rapidly sometimes that students fail to incorporate what they've learned and to think about it in terms of what they bring to the topic in the first place. Providing time for reflection and guiding students in developing tools for it is a wise teaching method. Recording the new learning in a journal is a way to provide reflection time for students.

Projects

Seeing a unit as a project is also very useful. It opens the door naturally to a multi-task approach to learning. Not only will the students learn about birds, they will have an opportunity to observe them, they can try their hands at drawing them, and they can learn to differentiate one from the other. It's easy to see how a lifetime interest in bird watching can take root in such a project, which is more effective than in simply reading about the topic and talking about it.

Skill 7.2 **Understands how to adjust lessons in response to student feedback; recognizing different communication techniques to enhance student understanding; understanding communication approaches that are sensitive to students' backgrounds (with respect to gender, language, and cultural differences).**

Years ago, students expected that teachers would put a letter grade at the top of their papers—and perhaps make grammatical corrections to written work. Those days are over. Teachers now are expected to provide feedback that actually helps students learn more.

The amount of time teachers spent grading work yielded little new learning for students. The fear of a low grade alone is not viewed as sufficient to let students know what they have done well and what they need additional work on. The old model of teachers teaching new knowledge and then expecting that students will learn it because of an assessment is gone. Students need deeper interaction, particularly as areas of knowledge and skills taught are becoming more complex.

In today's classrooms, students are both culturally and geographically diverse. There are typically 20-50 cultural languages spoken in school communities and the languages are representative of twice the cultural demographics of families who have immigrated to America. For example, in the Somalian community, there are an influx of family demographics that represent different cultural pockets from geographical areas that are representative of family clans and dialects. In a high school classroom, if a teacher states to a ELL (English Language Learner) student, "Your grammar needs to be worked on," that student may feel ostracized on the high school level to the extent of dropping out of school. Students, who are struggling to have access to a new beginning in American education, would find the above statement, personal and demeaning as they struggle to acquire opportunity and education in a foreign country immensely different from their origins.

Providing students with opportunities to share cultural stories and feel safe in today's classrooms will go a long way to creating cultural bridges and inclusion in school communities. Teachers who adjust lessons that include multicultural academic content and communication will create a global learning community that is reflective of the world experience for today's students. In typical high school classrooms, ELL learners are provided with comprehensive educational assessments in reading, writing and math before they are mainstreamed as 10th and 11th graders into mainstream classrooms and college oriented curriculums. Students are able to acquire proficient English skills to navigate upper level high school courses where every subject and assessment is written in English.

If teachers are really listening to student feedback, they will find that students are intuitive about learning and effective communication. Students will express areas of sensitivity and given encouragement by teacher and peers, students will expose their own gaps in learning. The safety of the learning environment is of utmost importance in providing teachers with the needed information on how to provide more effective lessons for student learning and teacher instructional adjustments.

High school teachers are continually providing feedback to students due to the nature of teaching that uses academic content expectations to promote a communicative and collaborative approach to student learning. Due to constant assessments for older students, the stakes are higher for circular feedback that must provide immediate feedback on student learning and teacher instructional practices.

The administrative process in every school community provides an evaluative tool for looking objectively at student learning and teaching impact on that learning. Focusing on student portfolio evaluations that include student work and assessment reports provide both administrator and teacher, a productive and objective evaluation tool for providing more effective curriculum instruction for students. Students on the high school level are more succinct in feedback expectations from teachers. The one question that students will ask is "What did I do wrong?" and the other question is "How should I fix it?" Students want concrete linear answers that address the "what" and the "how." For students, the ability to fix an improperly formatted essay or process to a mathematical word problem can be addressed with teacher answers that sound like "Reformat the paragraphs into shorter texts" or "provide a longer process of feedback to math word problems."

For students, the stakes are higher and equated into final grades and graduation. Grades are the concrete data that equate to college and beyond high school learning goals and future aspirations. High school students use journals to reflect on learning goals and objectives in classes from English to Science content areas. The collaborative process of group projects enables students to create rubric assessments that provide group feedback and individual reflection. Students who have active involvement in assessing their own work become more active in providing feedback to teachers on how to create projects and lessons that are more conducive to learning and academic success in the classroom.

See also Skill 6.5

Skill 7.3   Recognizes questioning methods that are bias-free and that are effective in maintaining student engagement and in encouraging risk taking and problem solving.

Teachers have to navigate the known and unknown triggers that students bring into the classroom from cultural, socioeconomic or psychological backgrounds. There will always be inherent bias, whether intended or not in the multi-faceted questions and issues that arise in classrooms. Recognizing that as a natural fact, will enable teachers to express to older students that sometimes trying to create methods that will not offend or dishonor is difficult, yet addressing issues that may come up during a classroom discussion is a healthy way of proactively dealing with sensitivity aspects of learning and teaching.

For experienced teachers, providing dialogue on questions that are possible triggers creates an atmosphere of learning and caring for both teacher and students. Students are able to explore and express cultural sensitivity issues to the class and get support and acknowledgment from peers and teachers regarding the validity of issues. Creating questions using diverse multicultural viewpoints is a known strategy for experience teachers. Implementing a myriad of multiple intelligences in creating questions is beneficial to structuring a curriculum that is bias free and proactive in encouraging student interaction and class participation.

See also Skill 2.4

Skill 7.4   Understands how to relate content to real-life situations.

See Skill 2.2

Skill 7.5   Understands how students can acquire information and concepts through a variety of modes and formats.

One of the most challenging aspects of teaching today is that while many students at all grade levels, K-12, still struggle with basic reading comprehension, the formats in which information is presented are expanding and multiplying. Just because information may be available in more seemingly friendly formats, such as the internet, does not mean that complex or advanced information will be any easier for students to comprehend. Therefore, it is imperative that teachers consider that comprehension, while still applied to textual sources (such as books, magazines, and newspapers), now needs to be applied to visual, audio, and multi-media sources, as well. We should not take for granted that students will be able to quickly comprehend, interpret, and evaluate these formats.

Realizing that comprehension of information from a variety of sources and modes needs to be taught explicitly, it is highly important that teachers help students learn how to *access* a variety of sources. It is often difficult for teachers, who may not have grown up with the internet (as opposed to their students), to realize that students are not as savvy at finding the *best* information as they think. Two primary examples illustrate this point. First, many students typically search in a very limited fashion on the internet. They are not as skilled at expanding the places they search for information (more specifically, the more *reputable* places). Second (and this is partly a result of the first), many sources they do find are low in quality. Therefore, in addition to helping students comprehend material from a variety of modes and formats, teachers must help students learn how to find quality material.

The idea that a variety of modes and formats can provide sufficient (or possibly better) information than traditional textual sources is a new, emerging concept in our highly networked world. Rather than going to a limited library, for example, a wider array of information is available online and through other audio-visual sources. This is both promising and problematic. While the modes and formats of sources increases (thus allowing wider access), we increase the chance that incorrect information is read and utilized.

Regardless of potential problems, students in all grades can learn how to view, read, and listen to a variety of sources through a variety of modes, thus "rounding out" concepts that might be presented narrowly or less comprehensibly in a textbook, for example. This is a unique skill to teach students, in fact. When information is not clear from one source, students can go to others to pick up different perspectives and examples of the concepts they are attempting to learn. Overall, our highly technological and integrated world has provided students with a vast array of opportunities to learn new concepts. It will take skilled teachers, though, to ensure that students learn how to use information tools appropriately and proficiently.

Skill 7.6   **Recognizes appropriate role(s) of the teacher in relation to a given instructional approach.**

The role of the classroom teacher will vary depending on the instructional approach used to achieve planned objectives. And the teacher's role may vary within a particular approach. Depending on the strategy employed, the teacher may sometimes be directly mentoring, lecturing or drilling students, as a class or in small groups; or, when working with the students individually or in small groups, the teacher may be serving more as a guide, encouraging and enabling students to make cognitive "discoveries" as new information is introduced and acquired skills are built upon. The following are examples of instructional approaches commonly employed:

Direct Instruction

"If the child hasn't learned, the teacher hasn't taught." This is the guiding philosophy for an educational technique known as Direct Instruction, a highly developed, scripted method of teaching that is fast-paced and provides for continual interaction between students and teacher. It has the following attributes:
- *Homogeneous Skill Grouping*: Students are grouped according to their levels of ability, rather than by any other factor.
- *Scripted Class Sessions*: Teachers use pre-designed scripts when teaching. The scripts (based on extensive research regarding student retention) are provided for the teacher, not prepared by the teacher.
- *Continual Student Interaction*: The scripted sessions are constructed in sequences of stimulus/response sets, wherein the teacher stimulates the class with a description of a concept, an illustration of the concept through an example, and finally a request that the class repeat the example. The class responds orally, usually as a group.
- Teaching to Mastery: The group does not move on until everyone in the group understands the material.

Lecture

The classroom lecture is a standard and traditional device used to impart information to the class as a whole. Generally, the classroom teacher prepares the lecture based on the detail of information necessary for the students to acquire prescribed skills at the level required to fulfill the educational objectives defined in the teacher's lesson plan. Of necessity, student questions and other interactions are delayed until the end of the lecture (or allowed only at planned intervals within the lecture) in order to avoid disruption in the flow of information which might cause a distraction or confusion for the students. The classroom teacher plans for, develops and delivers the lecture and should also employ follow-up devices (discussions, quizzes, etc.) to measure the effective acquisition of skills/knowledge by individual students.

Cooperative learning is a teaching strategy in which small teams, each with students of different levels of ability, use a variety of learning activities to improve their understanding of a subject. Each member of a team is responsible for learning and for helping teammates learn, thus creating an atmosphere of achievement. Students work through the assignment until all group members successfully understand and complete it. The teacher's role involves monitoring, prompting, advising and aiding the students to find the correct path, collectively, and achieve the prescribed objectives as a group—supportive and dependent on each individual in the group. Objectives of cooperative learning include,

- promoting student learning and academic achievement
- increasing student retention
- enhancing student satisfaction with the learning experience
- developing students' oral communication skills
- developing students' social skills
- promoting student self-esteem

Inquiry-Based Learning

"Tell me and I forget, show me and I remember, involve me and I understand." This statement serves as a philosophy for inquiry-based learning, where active inquiry leads to understanding. Understanding is knowing, and knowing (demonstrably) is skill/knowledge acquisition. The role of the teacher is to provide the framework and direction of instructional sessions, and to ensure that all students are involved and that inquiries are pertinent and purposeful. The teacher serves as monitor and mentor as well as guide. "Discovery" is available to the students, but may (of necessity) be prompted and directed by the teacher. The teacher also plans for skills/knowledge acquired through this method to be built upon, allowing students to internalize inquiry-based learning technique as a tool for continual intellectual development.

Interdisciplinary Instruction

Interdisciplinary instruction involves combining two (or more) disciplines into instructional units to aid and augment the students' understanding of issues/skills/practices in each discipline and to demonstrate how insights and skill acquisition in one area can assist academic achievement in other areas. Students are exposed to the concept that no field of knowledge exists in isolation to all others—and that comprehensive understanding is best achieved for all students when multiple perspectives are made available, presented and examined. It is considered possible and desirable to engage the student in any combination of academic disciplines appropriate to age and grade level so long as well defined objectives meeting the instructional requirements of each subject are incorporated in the lesson plan for each unit to be taught, and appropriate measures are incorporated to evaluate student progress within each subject area as well as within the interdisciplinary unit(s).

In classroom presentation and in student evaluation, the teacher's role is no different than for other instructional approaches. Quite to the contrary, any of the commonly accepted teaching approaches can be used in providing interdisciplinary instruction. The difference—for the teacher—is more apparent in the preparation and planning of instructional units and materials: identifying corresponding or complimentary skills from each discipline which are valuable to the students at their level; determining the appropriate means of evaluating skills acquisition that is verifiable within each discipline (according to the academic standards and objectives of each subject area); and attempting to transcend the level of understanding and abilities students would be expected to attain studying each subject in isolation.

Whole Group/Small Group Discussion, Hands-on Activity and Peer Tutoring

These instructional approaches are all intended to maximize student involvement in the learning process and enable them to actively assist one another in skill/knowledge acquisition. In practice, the teacher's role may be perceived as more passive than with traditional modes of instruction, serving more as a guide, encouraging and enabling students to make cognitive "discoveries" as new information is introduced and acquired skills are built upon. In actuality, these approaches can only be successfully applied in the classroom if the teacher has fully prepared for all activities and eventualities, well in advance. The teacher must have clearly defined objectives for each instructional activity and ensured that the students were fully aware of the purposes and academic objectives of these activities. The teacher must have identified/defined the appropriate measurement tools for each different activity. And, of course, the teacher will necessarily monitor the process, maintaining discipline and an appropriate learning environment for all students, ensure participation by all students, and actively prompt discussions and activities (as necessary) to keep students motivated and working towards the appropriate objectives.

Technology-Based Instruction, Individualized Instruction

There are many similarities between the previous group of instructional methods and technology-based instruction and individualized instruction; but the emphasis is on direct student activity and teacher guidance of the individual through the process. Technology-based instruction and/or individualized instruction is often successfully employed to meet the requirement for students within a diverse classroom to acquire the same academic skills (at the same levels). And this is often achieved through programmed learning instructional materials. The nature of these materials (and this approach to learning) allows for more individual attention than traditional classroom instruction, as each student starts from his or her evaluated level of need and works through the program to attain the skill level defined in the unit objective.

Programmed learning/instruction is not necessarily related to computer programming; although, many effective and creative, interactive, instructional programs are used with students on computers and computer networks. It is, rather, a program of instruction intended to bring a student who is at a predetermined level of skill or knowledge to the next level, with materials appropriate to realize pre-established objectives. While many approaches to programmed learning have been developed over the years, using a variety of media and incorporating sound pedagogical tenets, they still share common attributes. Generally, they are modular. A module is an instructional package teaching a single conceptual unit of subject matter. It is intended to individualize learning by enabling the student to master one unit of content before moving to another. Larger concepts or topics are broken down into useful and measurable component parts and each part is taught as a module. The modules are logically linked to bring the student, step-by-step, to the point of achieving all the objectives in the course.

Skill 7.7   Compares instructional approaches in terms of teacher and student responsibilities, expected student outcomes, and usefulness for achieving instructional purposes.

See Skill 7.1 and 7.6

COMPETENCY 8.0   UNDERSTAND A VARIETY OF METHODS FOR TEACHING LITERACY SKILLS THAT SUPPORT AND PROMOTE STUDENT ACHIEVEMENT.

Skill 8.1   Selects instructional strategies that help students use literacy skills (e.g., reading, writing, speaking, listening, viewing) as tools for learning.

The point of comprehension instruction is not necessarily to focus just on the text(s) students are using at the very moment of instruction, but rather to help them learn the strategies that they can use independently with any other text.

Some of the most common methods of teaching instruction are as follows:

- Summarization: This is where, either in writing or verbally, students go over the main point of the text, along with strategically chosen details that highlight the main point. This is not the same as paraphrasing, which is saying the same thing in different words. Teaching students how to summarize is very important as it will help them look for the most critical areas in a text, and in non-fiction. For example, it will help them distinguish between main arguments and examples. In fiction, it helps students to learn how to focus on the main characters and events and distinguish those from the lesser characters and events.

- Question answering: While this tends to be over-used in many classrooms, it is still a valid method of teaching students to comprehend. As the name implies, students answer questions regarding a text, either out loud, in small groups, or individually on paper. The best questions are those that cause students to have to think about the text (rather than just find an answer within the text).

- Question generating: This is the opposite of question answering, although students can then be asked to answer their own questions or the questions of peer students. In general, we want students to constantly question texts as they read. This is important because it causes students to become more critical readers. To teach students to generate questions helps them to learn the types of questions they can ask, and it gets them thinking about how best to be critical of texts.

- Graphic organizers: Graphic organizers are graphical representations of content within a text. For example, Venn diagrams can be used to highlight the difference between two characters in a novel or two similar political concepts in a Social Studies textbook. Or, a teacher can use flow-charts with students to talk about the steps in a process (for example, the steps of setting up a science experiment or the chronological events of a story). Semantic organizers are similar in that they graphically display information. The difference, usually, is that semantic organizers focus on words or concepts. For example, a word web can help students make sense of a word by mapping from the central word all the similar and related concepts to that word.

- Text structure: Often in non-fiction, particularly in textbooks, and sometimes in fiction, text structures will give important clues to readers about what to look for. Often, students do not know how to make sense of all the types of headings in a textbook and do not realize that, for example, the side-bar story about a character in history is not the main text on a particular page in the history textbook. Teaching students how to interpret text structures gives them tools in which to tackle other similar texts.

- Monitoring comprehension: Students need to be aware of their comprehension, or lack of it, in particular texts. So, it is important to teach students what to do when suddenly text stops making sense. For example, students can go back and re-read the description of a character. Or, they can go back to the table of contents or the first paragraph of a chapter to see where they are headed.

- Textual marking: This is where students interact with the text as they read. For example, armed with Post-it Notes, students can insert questions or comments regarding specific sentences or paragraphs within the text. This helps students to focus on the importance of the small things, particularly when they are reading larger works (such as novels in high school). It also gives students a reference point to go back into the text when they need to review something.

- Discussion: Small group or whole-class discussion stimulates thoughts about texts and gives students a larger picture of the impact of those texts. For example, teachers can strategically encourage students to discuss related concepts to the text. This helps students learn to consider texts within larger societal and social concepts, or teachers can encourage students to provide personal opinions in discussion. By listening to various students' opinions, this will help all students in a class to see the wide range of possible interpretations and thoughts regarding one text.

Many people mistakenly believe that the terms "research-based" or "research-validated" or "evidence-based" relate mainly to specific programs, such as early reading textbook programs. While research does validate that some of these programs are effective, much research has been conducted regarding the effectiveness of particular instructional strategies. In reading, many of these strategies have been documented in the report from the National Reading Panel (2000). However, just because a strategy has not been validated as effective by research does not necessarily mean that it is not effective with certain students in certain situations. The number of strategies out there far outweighs researchers' ability to test their effectiveness. Some of the strategies listed above have been validated by rigorous research, while others have been shown consistently to help improve students' reading abilities in localized situations. There simply is not enough space to list all the strategies that have been proven effective; just know that the above strategies are very commonly cited ones that work in a variety of situations.

It is also important to note that while the majority of research that has been presented to the public is at the elementary level, a significant amount of research has shown that many of the strategies that we use with younger students are indeed appropriate for older students. Let's take one example from above. Text structure at the elementary level might focus on general headings, as well as significant plot elements in a story. At the middle level, teachers can begin to teach about within-paragraph textual structures. For example, a comparison/contrast paragraph might start by demonstrating similarities between two concepts. It then could move on to discussing the differences of each concept one at a time. In other comparison/contrast paragraphs, differences might be discussed as groups. For a visual demonstration of these differences, examine these structures:

Example 1:

* Similarities of Concept A and Concept B
* All of the distinct features of Concept A
* All of the district features of Concept B

Example 2:

* One similarity between Concept A and Concept B
* Another similarity between Concept A and Concept B
* One *specific* difference between Concept A and Concept B
* Another *specific* difference between Concept A and Concept B

These types of things can be taught in the middle years and move into the high school years. They assist students in making sense of difficult informational content reading material.

Moving well into the high school years, text structure can be taught also by having students examine rhetorical structures in texts, such as noticing structures within sentences. For example, by using punctuation and various words, sentences can change the structures of paragraphs and whole essays.

So, to summarize, all of the reading comprehension skills that are taught to students in the elementary grades can easily be taught in the middle and high school grades at more advanced levels.

Skill 8.2   Understands the importance of promoting literacy in all areas of the curriculum by using a variety of resources (e.g., expository texts, electronic media)

Traditionally, reading and comprehension were taught through fiction. Today, reading and comprehension are taught through various media and from various genres.

Research shows that reading comprehension is drastically different when applied to fiction as it is to non-fiction. Simply put, although many skills cross over, we apply many different skills to each genre. For example, in non-fiction, we generally are searching for information. Language, while some of it may be pleasant and artistic, is not the primary point in reading non-fiction. Small subtleties in non-fiction are the result of artistic expression and may contribute less to meaning than in fiction. In fiction, we are more prone to pay attention to subtleties, small details, and language, as they give clues to meaning.

Research also shows that reading comprehension in print sources is very different than reading comprehension online. From a physical standpoint, our eyes work differently, our behaviors of movement are different, and our attention span is different. When we read online, we are more prone to move quickly between pages, skim, and scan. Although we do indeed do similar things with print text, we are more prone to read text in a continuous fashion.

Complete comprehension, whether we are reading online or from a book (or whether we are reading fiction or non-fiction), requires that we do certain things consistently. For complete comprehension, we would pay attention to details both large and small. We would also read everything carefully. We would not skip words, phrases, or sentences—or simply look for bold-printed words.

The truth is, though, that we do not necessarily need to read everything completely. Knowing when skimming and scanning are appropriate is a skill in itself, and it is worth teaching students at all grade levels. At elementary levels, we can first help students understand how to access information quickly from texts by skimming and scanning; then we can help them practice thorough reading and point out the differences.

At middle and high school grades, we can remind students of these skills, as well as have them put these skills into practice through research assignments. For example, let's say a high school student is completing a research assignment on a topic that is completely new to him or her. We would want that student to be able to get a good foundational understanding of the topic by reading both textual and multi-media sources through completely. Of course, we would have to help students understand which sources would be worth reading all the way through. Then, to add details and get a variety of new perspectives, we would need to teach them how to skim and scan additional text and online sources. Notice that skimming and scanning for these additional details is done after a foundation has been built. It is expressly for the purpose of adding new detail, rather than learning something new.

In summary, while sources of information are different, so too are the purposes we have for reading, researching, and accessing information. We must therefore teach students how to decide which methods to use according to the purposes they have, as well as the sources they are using.

Skill 8.3 Teaches students how to use, access, and evaluate information from various resources

It is necessary for each student to become knowledgeable about, and comfortable with using, all instructional resources. But the primary skill each student must acquire is the ability to identify the specific problem, issue or need to be addressed. If this can be understood and verbalized, then the student will be able to select the appropriate resource tool from among the available resources, once these have been introduced, used and understood.

As early as possible, we try to instill the skills necessary to make each child an independent researcher. The teaching faculty and library and support staff should work together to ensure that all students know the location of, and have access to, all appropriate learning resources, whether in the classroom, the school library, a lab or other resource center. The students should be made familiar with the layout of the resource center and understand the operation of any equipment available and suitable for their use. This could be anything from a card catalogue to a computer terminal or microfilm reader.

Working with each student to associate appropriate resources with identifiable needs is primary. Teaching effective and efficient use of each resource is the next concern. Time and practice (preferably, with prescribed exercises) should be expended on the rudiments of using explicit directives (such as tables of contents and indices or Web browsers) to make a necessary search expeditious, effective and even fun. Repeated practice with purpose is the surest method of instilling these skills in young students. Children are sometimes impulsive and impatient. Even after students have been taught proper reference and research procedure and technique, many will choose to just jump right into the text and slog back and forth through the pages, randomly, seeking an answer. While it can never be instinctive by nature, it should become second nature for the student (through practice) to always reference a table of contents and/or index to expedite the search, avoid frustration and make the task easier.

Examples

The Dictionary and the Encyclopedia
The dictionary is introduced to students by the teacher as a classroom resource at an early elementary level. They are shown how to access and practice using this dependable tool as an aid to alphabetizing and studying vocabulary for pronunciation, reading and writing. At the appropriate age/grade level, students will be introduced to the encyclopedia by the classroom teacher or school librarian as a compendium of knowledge and a principal tool for reference and research. As with all learning tools, students must be made aware of the purposes and processes of using the encyclopedia and the differences from other seemingly similar tools or applications. For instance, when deciding whether the dictionary or the encyclopedia is the appropriate tool for a specific task, students are shown that the comparison is in the access to information, by alphabetic ordering. The contrast is in the purpose as well as application of the resource. The dictionary is used to define the correct spelling, proper meaning and appropriate uses of a word. The encyclopedia is used to explain a topic, succinctly. While the dictionary is introduced to students as early as is practical (most often, by second grade), usually, the encyclopedia is introduced when students are ready to do supplemental reading or begin writing compositions or research papers with prescribed topics.

When the teacher introduces dictionary use to the class as a measurable skill, students will often be assigned drills to evaluate their skill level (using an abridged dictionary appropriate to the skill level of the students). Examples of these would be:

- Moving through the dictionary, the student will copy the first word and the last word for each letter of the alphabet.
- Working with a list of words—some of which are spelled correctly and some of which are spelled incorrectly—students will practice alphabetizing to the second letter of a word, and then to the third letter of a word, etc., by verifying the correct spelling in the dictionary and circling each correctly spelled word on the list.
- Working with a list of vowel sounds and consonant sounds, students will locate assigned words in the dictionary and match the words to the appropriate pronunciation of vowel or consonant.
- Working with randomly listed vocabulary words and randomly listed word definitions, students will verify the definition of each word, using the dictionary, and accurately match words with definitions on the list.
- Based on the matching of words and definitions (in the exercise above), students will create new sentences using the list words appropriately.
- Using the dictionary, students will correct for spelling and appropriate word use in short compositions of fellow classmates. The teacher should evaluate the accuracy of both the composer and the reviewer.

Teachers or librarians introducing encyclopedia use as a measurable skill will often assign and evaluate practice research projects for students. Examples of these would be:

- Working sequentially through a numbered list of randomly alphabetized, sample topics, the student will locate each sample topic in the encyclopedia and cite book and page number(s) for each one.
- Working sequentially through a numbered list of randomly alphabetized, sample topics, the student will select related subtopics from another list (or create his or her own list). The student will locate each subtopic in the encyclopedia and cite book and page number(s) for each one.
- Working sequentially through a numbered list of randomly alphabetized, sample topics, the student will identify and list valid cross references, locate these within the encyclopedia and cite book and page number(s) for each one.

Skill 8.4 **Identifies ways to support students' development of content-area reading skills.**

The educational community has not done the best job at transitioning students into reading tasks that require accessing information, making real-world judgments, or comprehending directions. Typically, children are taught to read with fiction, and then suddenly, we hand them science and social science textbooks and believe that they will be able to handle the material successfully. While it is a bit of an exaggeration to say that teachers do not use non-fiction in younger grades, it is true that many students are completely unprepared to use textbooks with complete ease. Furthermore, when we start to assign research projects in upper elementary, middle school, and/or high school, we forget that students not only struggle with comprehending non-fiction sources, they also struggle with assessing the reliability of sources. This is why, in these days where kids are often better at using the internet than some of their teachers, the sources of students' research projects are not always reliable. While they can easily navigate around the web, they do not always have the ability to decide whether a website is professional or not.

The reason for this is simple: inexperience with having to judge sources, combined with the lack of instruction regarding the proper selection of sources. To go a bit deeper, another reason for this is that students do not always know strategies for reading content-area material. Let's take middle school subjects, for example. The English-Language Arts teacher, who instructs students in the elements of fiction, such as character, setting, and plot, is teaching her students strategies for understanding fiction. Likewise, that same teacher who conducts lessons on rhyme and imagery in poetry is teaching her students the strategies for reading poetry. When do students get the opportunity to study the ways in which we come to understand the material in the science textbook or the math textbook? Too often, we assume that they will naturally be able to read those materials. And too often, we then find that our students are completely lost in a science textbook. With today's textbooks, the struggle to make sense of the material goes further: To supposedly keep students' attention, textbooks contain flashy graphics, side-bars with somewhat related information, discussion questions, vocabulary entries, etc. Surprisingly, some students simply do not know which parts of the text are required reading and which are peripheral.

To improve this situation, it is strongly recommended that teachers explicitly teach the strategies needed to make sense of non-fiction sources. Some of the strategies are as follows:

- Text structure: This refers to both the arrangement of a book (e.g., chapters, sub-headings, etc.) as well as the method of paragraphs (e.g., a paragraph that introduces a concept and explains it, versus one that compares and contrasts one concept with another).

- Summarization: This is much harder for students than it may seem. Too often, students believe that summarization is simply the re-telling of information that has been read. In actuality, summarization requires that the student identify the most important details, identify the main point, and highlight the pieces of a text that give light to that main point.

- Source identification: Although this isn't a term that gets used too much, the concept is very important. Teachers must instruct students explicitly in methods of determining whether a website, for example, is reliable or not. Methods for doing so include discussing author credentials, page layout, website links, etc.

- Vocabulary: Teachers need to train students to look up words they are unfamiliar with or use textbook-provided glossaries. When students are unfamiliar with vocabulary used in textbooks, comprehension is much slower.

- Text annotation: Students will be more active readers if they interact with the text they are reading in some fashion. Marking texts can help students identify for themselves what concepts they are already familiar with, what concepts they are unclear about, or what concepts interest them.

- Background knowledge: Students who find a way to activate background knowledge will be far more successful with reading non-fiction than those who do not. This is because background knowledge serves as a place to organize and attach new knowledge more quickly.

While there are plenty more strategies that can be used, just remember that students need explicit instruction in understanding and accessing non-fiction material.

In particular, we can help middle and high school students better comprehend textbooks. Textbooks today often are written and designed so that they are visually stimulating. While textbook pages may *look* more interesting now than they did in generations past, they are not necessarily easier to read. There are two reasons for this. First, textbooks now have more information available in which to synthesize and present to students than in the past. As the information in various fields expands rapidly—and textbook publishers feel the need to include as much information as possible—textbooks become more and more convoluted and confusing. Teachers must therefore be very discerning in how they assign textbook readings. They must also use the strategies listed above to help students get through the material more successfully.

The second reason why textbooks are not as easy to read is indeed the presentation designed to make the pages look more interesting. The design may confuse students on which section of a page's text is most important, for example. Often, bits and pieces of information, as well as questions, "quick-facts", and other informational "side-bars" may interfere with the primary text. Teachers must remind students which sections are most important and which sections are peripheral.

In general, teaching students to read nonfiction in content areas at any level takes great skill; and it is not a skill reserved for the Language Arts teacher alone!

Skill 8.5   Demonstrates knowledge of ways to address the literacy needs of all students, including those whose primary language is not English.

The primary responsibility of the classroom teacher is to ensure that all aspects of the educational process, and all information necessary to master specified skills, are readily accessible by all students in the classroom. In the classroom, the teacher must actively promote inclusion and devise presentations which address commonalities among heterogeneous groups. In the development of lesson plans and presentation formats, this should be evident in the concepts and in the language used (e.g., incorporating ideas and phrases which suggest "we" rather than "they" whenever possible).

Initially, the teacher must take the time to know each student as an individual, and demonstrate a sincere interest in each student. For example, it is important to know the correct spelling and pronunciation of each student's name, and any preference in how the student would like to be addressed. Teachers should plan time for interaction in the classroom, when the teacher and the class can become familiar with each student's interests and experiences. This will help the teacher and the students avoid making assumptions based on any individual's background or appearance.

The prescribed teaching material in a given subject area will usually provide an adequate format appropriate to the grade level and the diversity of a general student population. By assuring that any additional content or instructional aids used in classroom presentation are thematically the same as the prescribed material, the teacher can usually assume these will also be appropriate. But the teacher is the final arbiter regarding content, format and presentation in the classroom. So the teacher must exercise judgment when reviewing all classroom materials, lesson plans, presentations and activities against set criteria. Consider the following:

Offensive: Anything which might be considered derogatory regarding any individual or group; any comment or material which is insensitive to any nationality, religion, culture, race, family structure, etc. Regardless of the composition of a particular classroom, negativism about any group harbors an acceptance of such negativism and contributes to a "them" versus "us" attitude.

Exclusive: Anything which ignores or nullifies the needs, rights or value of an individual or any group; anything which stratifies society, placing some group or groups above others in significance.

<u>Inappropriate</u>: Below or beyond the suitable comprehension level; imprecise, inadequate for mastery of specific skills within the subject matter; fails to provide for accurately measurable skill acquisition.

The teacher should actively work to broaden the students' sense of "we," even beyond the classroom and the local community, to foster a sense of all people as "we." For example, while avoiding the use of colloquialisms or local slang within lesson presentation, the teacher would demonstrate an understanding and acceptance of the richness and variety of ways in which people communicate.

When planning instruction in literacy for a diverse group, incorporate teaching through the use of perspective. There is always more than one way to "see" or approach a problem, an example, a process, a fact or event, or any learning situation. Varying approaches for instruction helps to maintain the students' interest in the material and enables the teacher to address the diverse needs of individuals to comprehend the material.

The requirement for students within a diverse classroom to acquire the same academic skills (at the same levels) can sometimes be achieved with programmed learning instructional materials. A good deal of useful material is in publication. Professional teachers familiar with the format have often created their own modules for student use, to be incorporated within their lesson planning.

Diversity in classroom makeup may not be as distinctive as race and ethnicity, gender and so forth. Students who are physically or intellectually challenged may also add diversity within a general student population. A student population including members from varying socioeconomic situations also provides diversity. All students must be included in the learning process and all students can achieve literacy. Acceptance of this diversity, by students, and any specific requirements necessary to aid individual students to accomplish on a par with classmates, must be incorporated in lesson planning, teacher presentation and classroom activities. For example, access to technology and media, generally, may vary greatly within the student population. In planning classroom work, homework assignments and other projects, the teacher must take this into account. First, be knowledgeable about the resources available to the students, directly, within the school, the library system and the community. Be sure that any issues which might restrict a student's access (physical impediments, language difficulties, expenses, etc.) are addressed. Secondly, never plan for work or assignments where every student would not have equal access to information and technology. As in all aspects of education, each student must have an equal opportunity to succeed.

Curriculum objectives and instructional strategies may be inappropriate and unsuccessful when presented in a single format which relies on the student's understanding and acceptance of the values and common attributes of a specific culture which is not his or her own. Planning, devising and presenting material from a multicultural perspective can enable the teacher in a culturally diverse classroom to ensure that all the students achieve the stated, academic objective. Even when the student population is largely culturally homogeneous, teaching with cultural perspective is always an asset to student comprehension and learning. When instructing on appropriate use of phonemes, for example, the teacher should be aware (and may find it relevant to classroom presentation or for helping individual students) that phonemes are sounded and applied differently in a variety of cultures, and their application in the English language may be a transitional process for some students.

For the classroom teacher planning such activities, there is a tremendous variety of single medium and multimedia, modular planning and instructional packages available through educational publishers. Not to be overlooked are the programs and activities developed by colleagues within the school system and beyond (via the Internet, for example).

In their article, Meeting the Needs of English Language Learners (copyright 2000, National Council of Teachers of English), David and Yvonne Freedman stated, "Teachers working with multilingual and multicultural students also need to be informed about second language acquisition theory and research and issues related to diversity. In addition, they need to learn about materials that support their students' first languages and are culturally relevant. Most important, they need to develop effective methods for teaching students whose backgrounds and experiences are different from their own."

See also Skill 8.1

COMPETENCY 9.0   UNDERSTAND STRATEGIES THAT ENCOURAGE
MOTIVATION AND POSITIVE BEHAVIOR
NECESSARY TO THE STRUCTURE AND
MANAGEMENT OF A CLASSROOM ENVIRONMENT
THAT PROMOTES STUDENT LEARNING AND
POSITIVE SOCIAL INTERACTIONS.

Skill 9.1   Identifies procedures for enhancing student interest and
helping students find their own motivation (e.g., relating
concepts presented in the classroom to students' everyday
needs, experiences, and cultural backgrounds, encouraging
student-initiated activities; highlighting connections between
academic learning and the world outside the classroom).

When students are interested in the lesson, their interest and motivation for
learning increases. Teachers should provide opportunities so students may work
toward becoming self-directed, and therefore, self-motivated, learners.

Skill knowledge, strategy use, motivation, and personal interests are all factors
that influence individual student success. Success-oriented activities are tasks
that are selected to meet the individual needs and interests of the student.
During the time a student is learning a new skill, tasks should be selected so that
the student will be able to earn a high percentage of correct answers during the
teacher questioning and seatwork portions of the lesson. Later, the teacher
should also include work that challenges students to apply what they have
learned and stimulate their thinking.

In the success-oriented classroom, mistakes are viewed as a natural part of the
learning process. The teacher can also show that adults make mistakes by
correcting errors without getting unduly upset. The students feel safe to try new
things because they know that they have a supportive environment and can
correct their mistakes.

Activities that promote student success:
a) are based on useful, relevant content that is clearly specified, and
organized for easy learning
b) allow sufficient time to learn the skill and is selected for high rate of
success
c) allow students the opportunity to work independently, self-monitor, and set
goals
d) provide for frequent monitoring and corrective feedback
e) include collaboration in group activities or peer teaching

Students with learning problems often attribute their successes to luck or ease of the task. Their failures are often blamed on their supposed lack of ability, difficulty of the task, or the fault of someone else. Successful activities, attribution retraining, and learning strategies can help these students to discover that they can become independent learners. When the teacher communicates the expectation that the students can be successful learners and chooses activities that will help them be successful, achievement is increased.

Develop a plan for progression from directed to self-directed activity

Learning progresses in stages from initial acquisition, when the student needs a lot of teacher guidance and instruction to adaptation, when the student can apply what he or she has learned to new situations outside the classroom. As students progress through the stages of learning, the teacher gradually decreases the amount of direct instruction and guidance and encourages the student to function independently. The ultimate goal of the learning process is to teach students how to be independent and apply their knowledge. A summary of these states and their features appears on the next page.

State	Teacher Activity	Emphasis
Initial Acquisition	Provide rationale Guidance Demonstration Modeling Shaping Cueing	Errorless learning Backward chaining (working from the final product backward through the steps) Forward chaining (proceeding through the steps to a final product)
Advanced Acquisition	Feedback Error correction Specific directions	Criterion evaluation Reinforcement and reward for accuracy
Proficiency	Positive reinforcement Progress monitoring Teach self-management Increased teacher expectations	Increase speed or performance to the automatic level with accuracy Set goals Self-management
Maintenance	Withdraw direct reinforcement Retention and memory Over learning Intermittent schedule of reinforcement	Maintain high level of performance Mnemonic techniques Social and intrinsic reinforcement
Generalization	Corrective feedback	Perform skill in different times and places
Adaptation	Stress independent problem-solving	Independent problem-solving methods No direct guidance or direct instruction

Particularly at the high school level, while basic skills still need to be taught and reinforced, teachers cannot forget how intellectually curious teenagers are. When teachers forget that their teenage students are interested in academic and intellectual ideas, the students often are offended. They want to be challenged, and they want the opportunity to explore complex ideas. Often, their curiosities are based on trying to understand the world around them. So while the curriculum calls for teaching about specific scientific concepts (and it may be tempting to teach strictly to the concept in the most efficient manner possible), when the concepts are taught *through* experiences and curiosities students have about their world, they often will learn the concepts better—and they will be more interested in process.

As teachers, we learn about students' interests by asking. We might, for example, open up discussions about appealing and interesting ideas related to the concepts we are about to teach. We might also ask students to write briefly about their experiences or background knowledge related to the concepts we are about to teach. In general, when we work to learn from our students, we find the types of things that will best help *them* learn from *us.*

The very idea of classroom discussion—as simplistic as it sounds—is often overlooked and underused by most teachers. Yet many students find open-ended discussion to be a highly motivating activity. They want to be able to express viewpoints and opinions to their peers and teachers, and whole-class open-ended discussion allows it. For the teacher's purpose, it helps shape ways in which concepts can be approached. For example, common experiences students have, when brought up in class discussion, can serve as examples later when the more difficult concepts are brought up through direct instruction.

Skill 9.2 Analyzes the effects of using various motivational strategies (e.g., intrinsic and extrinsic) in given situations.

As a rule, teachers should strive to encourage intrinsic motivation for students' learning. To do so lessens the need to use extrinsic motivators, such as frivolous rewards and harsh punishments.

The best way to encourage intrinsic motivation is to engage students in the learning. Engagement happens most when students work with material that is of greatest interest to them and if they feel there is a useful application for such material. For example, teachers will notice intrinsic motivation in reading when students have found books that they relate to. When teachers believe that certain students just will not read, often (though not always), those students have not found books that they like.

The extrinsic motivator of grades can be a particularly large challenge for well-meaning high school teachers who have college-bound students. Such students may not care as much about the learning as they do about the grades, so that their college applications look more competitive. Unfortunately, across the country, this has resulted in very troubling behavior. Plagiarism and cheating have been noticed in high schools everywhere. While teachers may want to encourage students to learn for the sake of the learning itself, they must contend with students who have been trained to "win at all costs." Teachers can therefore use many strategies—NOT to eradicate the very act of cheating, for example—but to encourage students to explore topics that are of interest to them or to create more meaningful, authentic assessments. Authentic assessments are those in which students have to use new learning in a real-world, deeply meaningful way.

Finally, it must be noted that punishment as an extrinsic motivator, while necessary at some times, often creates greater problems in the future. Students who feel like they are constantly punished into better behavior or to do better academically lose interest in pleasing teachers, acting appropriately, or learning. It is always better, whenever possible, for teachers to work at engaging students first, and then punishing if all options have been exhausted.

See also Skill 3.2

Skill 9.3   Recognizing factors and situations that tend to promote or diminish student motivation

See Skill 9.2 and 9.4

Skill 9.4   Analyzes teacher-student interactions with regard to motivation and behavior issues (e.g., communicating expectations and standards of behavior, providing feedback, building student self-esteem and classroom community).

Student-student and teacher-student interactions play a significant role in a positive classroom climate. When interactions among classroom members are encouraging, learning becomes a more natural and genuine process. Cold or routine interactions discourage questioning, critical thinking and useful discussion. Teachers should make every effort to be available to their students, as well as provide natural, collaborative opportunities for students in order to strengthen classroom interactions. Reflection, observations and asking for feedback regarding one's classroom interactions (perhaps during a yearly observation) will help teachers to analyze the effectiveness of their classroom's interactions.

The most important component in probing for student understanding is trust. Only if students trust their teacher will the communications process yield such things as the level of understanding a student has attained on any topic. If that component is in place, then creative questioning, which requires planning ahead, can sometimes reveal what the teacher needs to know. So can writing exercises that focus not on correctness but on a recording of the student's thoughts on a topic. Sometime assuring the student that only the teacher will see what is written is helpful in freeing students to reveal their own thoughts. When a new unit is introduced, including vocabulary lessons related to the unit can help students find the words they need to talk or write about the topic.

If a teacher can help students to take responsibility for their own ideas and thoughts, much has been accomplished. They will only reach that level in a non-judgmental environment, an environment that doesn't permit criticism of the ideas of others and that accepts any topic for discussion that is in the realm of appropriateness. Success in problem solving boosts students' confidence and makes them more willing to take risks, and the teacher must provide those opportunities for success.

At the high school level, students often say that they want to be treated as adults. Obviously, teenagers are not adults, but more than anything, they want to be taken seriously, and they want adults' respect. Of course, they are simply learning how to be adults, and every time we treat them as children, they are inclined to take offense. For many students, that offense results in behavior that is indeed childlike. So, when we treat teenagers like children, they very well may act like children. When we treat teenagers with respect, they are more likely (though not always, of course) to act responsibly and with maturity.

In addition to basic adult-student communication, high school students want to be part of an engaging classroom environment that stimulates thought and allows self-expression. When we must teach basic skills, we must do so with an attitude of respect, rather than one that belittles students.

It must be noted that while we should strive to treat teenagers with respect, we in no way should limit our rules and standards for behavior. Without standards for appropriate conduct, teenagers are not sure where the limits are drawn. This is where teenagers will most resemble younger children. They need (and often want) limits placed on their behaviors. When teachers (and parents) do not uphold those standards, teenagers respect them less.

Skill 9.5   Analyzes relationships between classroom management strategies and student learning, attitudes, and behaviors.

Classroom management plans should be in place when the school year begins. Developing a management plan takes a proactive approach—that is, decide what behaviors will be expected of the class as a whole, anticipate possible problems, and teach the behaviors early in the school year. Behavior management techniques should focus on positive procedures that can be used at home as well at school. Involving the students in the development of the classroom rules lets the students know the rationale for the rules, and allows them to assume responsibility for the rules because they had a part in developing them. Once the rules are established, enforcement and reinforcement for following the rules should begin right away.

Consequences should be introduced when the rules are introduced, clearly stated, and understood by all of the students. The severity of the consequence should match the severity of the offense and must be enforceable. The teacher must apply the consequence consistently and fairly; so the students will know what to expect when they choose to break a rule.

Like consequences, students should understand what rewards to expect for following the rules. The teacher should never promise a reward that cannot be delivered, and follow through with the reward as soon as possible. Consistency and fairness is also necessary for rewards to be effective. Students will become frustrated and give up if they see that rewards and consequences are not delivered timely and fairly.

About four to six classroom rules should be posted where students can easily see and read them. These rules should be stated positively, and describe specific behaviors so they are easy to understand. Certain rules may also be tailored to meet target goals and IEP requirements of individual students. (For example, a new student who has had problems with leaving the classroom may need an individual behavior contract to assist him or her with adjusting to the class rule about remaining in the assigned area.) As the students demonstrate the behaviors, the teacher should provide reinforcement and corrective feedback. Periodic "refresher" practice can be done as needed, for example, after a long holiday or if students begin to "slack off." A copy of the classroom plan should be readily available for substitute use, and the classroom aide should also be familiar with the plan and procedures.

The teacher should clarify and model the expected behavior for the students. In addition to the classroom management plan, a management plan should be developed for special situations, (i.e., fire drills) and transitions (i.e., going to and from the cafeteria). Periodic review of the rules, as well as modeling and practice, may be conducted as needed, such as after an extended school holiday.

Procedures that use social humiliation, withholding of basic needs, pain, or extreme discomfort should never be used in a behavior management plan. Emergency intervention procedures used when the student is a danger to himself or others are not considered behavior management procedures. Throughout the year, the teacher should periodically review the types of interventions being used and assess their effectiveness, and make revisions as needed for the best interests of the child.

Although the above procedures can indeed be used at the high school level, it is additionally important to note that rules and standards should demonstrate to students that students are respected. Logic is very important in setting standards for high school students. They need to see that a rule is designed specifically for a pragmatic purpose, rather than just the whim of a teacher who wants things a certain way. Furthermore, at the high school level, certain negative behaviors are not as prevalent as they are at the elementary and middle school levels. For example, students in high school are not as willing to be disruptive in class (due to peer social pressures). Yet, they may be less inclined to participate, and disruptions such as tardiness and absenteeism can be more prevalent. Rules must be stated for these purposes, and communication must be used (with students, parents, and school administrators) when tardiness and absenteeism becomes highly noticeable. But once again, respect is the key. Teachers should communicate with students and ask them to explain their actions. Often, students are not used teachers being "real" with them—but they certainly do appreciate it!

Skill 9.6   Demonstrates knowledge of strategies for managing the instructional environment to promote productivity, optimize students' time on-task, manage disruptive behaviors, and establish, communicate, and implement classroom procedures.

A teacher's ultimate goal is ensuring that students learn. And because student learning depends on many factors (including the engagement students have in a lesson, specific "teachable" moments, and other issues that arise in the learning environment), it is important that teachers pay close attention for things that might reduce optimal learning.

Here's an example: A science teacher has prepared a lesson on a very difficult science concept. Knowing that the concept is not simple, the teacher develops a lesson that she believes is very engaging. However, halfway through the lesson, the teacher notices that students are either puzzled or bored. Realizing that continuing the lesson "as is" will not promote deep learning, the teacher immediately changes the situation and alters the lesson to promote better engagement and understanding.

Or, the science teacher may notice that a particular student question draws great interest among other students. The question is sparked by the content, related to science, but not part of the teacher's learning objective. That teacher would be irresponsible to just move forward and ignore the question. To ignore it would say to students that learning is supposed to be boring and that school is not supposed to feed the intellectual interests of students. Assessing a sense of curiosity in the students, the teacher engages students in a brief answer to the question.

Let's say the science teacher incorporated a brief experiment as a learning exercise for the particular learning objectives in that lesson. Walking around watching students, she notices that students are making incorrect attributions to the things they are finding in their experiments. The science teacher pauses the experiment and re-teaches a simple concept. Students can then proceed to finish the experiment.

These examples demonstrate how an expert teacher adjusts lessons to meet the learning needs of students on an on-going basis. It proves that any well-planned lesson still may need adjustment. It also shows that the effective teacher will look for ways to make a good lesson better—even if it's in the middle of the lesson delivery!

Instructional momentum requires an organized system for material placement and distribution. Inability to find an overhead transparency, a necessary chart page, or the handout worksheet for the day not only stops the momentum, but is very irritating to students. Disorganization of materials frustrates both teacher and students. Effective teachers deal with daily classroom procedures efficiently and quickly because then students will spend the majority of class time engaged in academic tasks which will likely result in higher achievement.

In the lower grades an organized system uses a "classroom helper" for effective distribution and collection of books, equipment, supplies, etc. At higher grade levels, the teacher is concerned with materials such as textbooks, written instructional aids, worksheets, computer programs, etc., which must be produced, maintained, distributed, and collected for future use. One important consideration is the production of sufficient copies of duplicated materials to satisfy classroom needs. Another is the efficient distribution of worksheets and other materials. The teacher may decide to hand out materials as students are in their learning sites (desks, etc.), or to have distribution materials at a clearly specified place (or small number of places) in the classroom. In any case, there should be firmly established procedures, completely understood by student for receiving classroom materials.

An effective teacher will also consider the needs and abilities of her students when developing routines or a daily schedule. For routines, a teacher might motivate a low-achieving student with a coveted task (such as taking down the attendance sheet or a recommendation for Safety Patrol) in order to increase confidence in that child. This increased confidence could lead to an increased interest in school and improved learning. Likewise, a teacher should also consider the needs of his or her students when developing the aspects of the daily schedule. For instance, if faced with a "hard to calm down" group, a teacher might schedule quiet reading time after recess. Being aware of their students' trends and characteristics in developing a classroom routine can significantly impact student learning.

Using Time Wisely

Effective teachers use class time efficiently. This results in higher student subject engagement and will likely result in more subject matter retention. One way teachers use class time efficiently is through a smooth transition from one activity to another; this activity is also known as "management transition." Management transition is defined as "teacher shifts from one activity to another in a systemic, academically oriented way." One factor that contributes to efficient management transition is the teacher's management of instructional material. Effective teachers gather their materials during the planning stage of instruction. Doing this, a teacher avoids flipping through things looking for the items necessary for the current lesson. Momentum is lost and student concentration is broken when this occurs.

Additionally, teachers who keep students informed of the sequencing of instructional activities maintain systematic transitions because the students are prepared to move on to the next activity. For example, the teacher says, "When we finish with this guided practice together, we will turn to page twenty-three and each student will do the exercises. I will then circulate throughout the classroom helping on an individual basis. Okay, let's begin." Following an example such as this will lead to systematic smooth transitions between activities because the students will be turning to page twenty-three when the class finishes the practice without a break in concentration.

Another method that leads to smooth transitions is to move students in groups and clusters rather than one by one. This is called "group fragmentation." For example, if some students do seat work while other students gather for a reading group, the teacher moves the students in pre-determined groups. Instead of calling the individual names of the reading group, which would be time consuming and laborious, the teacher simply says, "Will the blue reading group please assemble at the reading station. The red and yellow groups will quietly do the vocabulary assignment I am now passing out." As a result of this activity, the classroom is ready to move on in a matter of seconds rather than minutes.

Additionally, the teacher may employ academic transition signals, defined as academic transition signals— "a teacher utterance that indicate[s] movement of the lesson from one topic or activity to another by indicating where the lesson is and where it is going." For example, the teacher may say, "That completes our description of clouds; now we will examine weather fronts." Like the sequencing of instructional materials, this keeps the student informed on what is coming next so they will move to the next activity with little or no break in concentration.

Transition refers to changes in class activities that involve movement. Examples are:

(a)   breaking up from large group instruction into small groups for learning centers and small-group instructions

(b)   classroom to lunch, to the playground, or to elective classes

(c)   finishing reading at the end of one period and getting ready for math the next period

(d)   emergency situations such as fire drills

Successful transitions are achieved by using proactive strategies. Early in the year, the teacher pinpoints the transition periods in the day and anticipates possible behavior problems, such as students habitually returning late from lunch. After identifying possible problems with the environment or the schedule, the teacher plans proactive strategies to minimize or eliminate those problems. Proactive planning also gives the teacher the advantage of being prepared, addressing behaviors before they become problems, and incorporating strategies into the classroom management plan right away. Transition plans can be developed for each type of transition and the expected behaviors for each situation taught directly to the students.

Transitions at the high school level are sometimes problematic, as students move from class to class and often have only forty to sixty minutes per class. While short class periods and these frequent disruptions can pose problems for the learning of complex concepts, teachers can design their lessons so that time is used to its fullest potential. When a teacher has very distinct, rapid-paced (yet in-depth) lessons that require active thinking and learning on a daily basis, students will quickly learn that this teacher means business! Class time is valued and is used to its fullest extent. Homework given is appropriate and adds to learning. No busy work is ever given, and the teacher stays involved in all aspects of the class period. Such a teacher will notice that students are on task more often and disruptive much less often. They will also notice students learning more in such a dynamic environment.

SUBAREA III.   THE PROFESSIONAL ENVIRONMENT

COMPETENCY 10.0   UNDERSTAND HOW TO ESTABLISH AND MAINTAIN
                   EFFECTIVE HOME-SCHOOL RELATIONSHIPS AND
                   SCHOOL-COMMUNITY INTERACTIONS THAT
                   SUPPORT STUDENT LEARNING.

Skill 10.1   Recognizes strategies for initiating and maintaining effective
              communication between the teacher and parents/guardians,
              including those from diverse backgrounds, and recognizing
              factors that may facilitate communication in given situations
              (including teacher conferences with parents/guardians).

The support of the parent is an invaluable aid in the educational process. It is in
the best interests of child, parent, and teacher for there to be cooperation and
mutual support between parent and teacher. One of the teacher's professional
responsibilities is to establish and maintain effective communication with parents.
A few basic techniques to pursue are oral communication (phone calls), written
communication in the form of general information classroom newsletters, notes to
the parent of a particular child, and parent-teacher conferences.

Teachers should share items of interest with parents, including but not limited to,
classroom rules and policies, class schedules and routines, homework
expectations, communication procedures, conferences plans, and other similar
information. Much of this can be done in a newsletter format sent home early in
the school year. It is imperative that all such written communications be error
free. It is a good idea to have another teacher read your letter before you send it
out. Good writing and clear communication are learned skills and require time
and effort to develop.

When you find it necessary to communicate (whether by phone, letter, or in
person) with a parent regarding a concern about a student, allow yourself a
"cooling off" period before making contact with the parent. It is important that you
remain professional and objective. Your purpose for contacting the parent is to
elicit support and additional information that may have a bearing on the student's
behavior or performance. Be careful that you do not demean the child and do not
appear antagonistic or confrontational. Be aware that the parent is likely to be
quite uncomfortable with the bad news and will respond best if you take a
cooperative, problem solving approach to the issue. It is also a nice courtesy to
notify parents of positive occurrences with their children. The teacher's
communication with parents should not be limited to negative items.

Skill 10.2   Describes strategies for using community resources to enrich learning experiences.

The community is a vital link to increasing learning experiences for students. Community resources can supplement the minimized and marginal educational resources of school communities. With state and federal educational funding becoming increasingly subject to legislative budget cuts, school communities welcome the financial support that community resources can provide in terms of discounted prices on high end supplies (e.g. computers, printers, and technology supplies), along with providing free notebooks, backpacks and student supplies for low income students who may have difficulty obtaining the basic supplies for school.

Community stores can provide cash rebates and teacher discounts for educators in struggling school districts and compromised school communities. Both professionally and personally, communities can enrich the student learning experiences by including the following support strategies:

- Provide programs that support student learning outcomes and future educational goals
- Create mentoring opportunities that provide adult role models in various industries to students interested in studying in that industry
- Provide financial support for school communities to help low-income or homeless students begin the school year with the basic supplies
- Develop paid internships with local university students to provide tutorial services for identified students in school communities who are having academic and social difficulties processing various subject areas.
- Providing parent-teen-community forums to create public voice of change in communities
- Offer parents without computer or Internet connection stipends to purchase technology to create equitable opportunities for students to do research and complete word.doc paper requirements.
- Stop in classrooms and ask teachers and students what's needed to promote academic progress and growth.

Community resources are vital in providing that additional support to students, school communities and families struggling to remain engaged in declining educational institutions competing for federal funding and limited district funding. The commitment that a community shows to its educational communities is a valuable investment in the future. Community resources that are able to provide additional funding for tutors in marginalized classrooms or help schools reduce classrooms of students needing additional remedial instruction directly impact educational equity and facilitation of teaching and learning for both teachers and students.

Skill 10.3   Recognizes various ways in which school personnel, local citizens, and community institutions (e.g., businesses, cultural institutions, colleges and universities, social agencies) can work together to promote a sense of community that will support student learning.

The bridge to effective learning for students begins with a collaborative approach by all stakeholders that support the educational needs of students. Underestimating the power and integral role of the community institutions in impacting the current and future goals of students can carry high stakes for students beyond the high school years when they are competing for college access, student internships, and entry level jobs in the community. Researchers have shown that school involvement and connections with community institutions have greater retention rates of students graduating and seeking higher education experiences. The current disconnect and autonomy that has become commonplace in today's society must be reevaluated in terms of promoting tomorrow's citizens.

When community institutions provide students and teachers with meaningful connections and input, the commitment is apparent in terms of volunteering, loyalty and professional promotion. Providing students with placements in leadership positions such as the ASB (Associated Student Body); the PTSA (Parent Teacher Student Association); School Boards; neighborhood sub-committees addressing political or social issues; or government boards that impact and influence school communities creates an avenue for students to explore ethical, participatory, collaborative, transformational leadership that can be applied to all areas of a student's educational and personal life.

Community liaisons provide students with opportunities to experience accountability and responsibility so that students learn about life and how organizations work with effective communication and teamwork to accomplish goals and objectives. Teaching students skills of inclusion, social and environmental responsibility and then creating public forums that represent student voice, foster student interest and give them access to developing and reflecting on individual opinions and understanding the dynamics of the world around them.

When a student sees that the various support systems are in place and consistently working as a team to effectively provide resources and avenues of academic promotion and accountability, students have no fear of taking risks to grow by becoming a teen voice on a local committee about "Teen Violence" or volunteering in a local hospice for young children with terminal diseases. The links to community institutions provide role-models to help the student become an integral and vital member of the real world.

COMPETENCY 11.0 UNDERSTAND PROFESSIONAL ROLES, EXPECTATIONS, AND LEGAL AND ETHICAL RESPONSIBILITIES OF ARIZONA EDUCATORS.

Skill 11.1 Understands how professional growth and development opportunities and personal reflection enhance teaching effectiveness.

Enhancing one's teaching effectiveness

Professional development opportunities for teacher performance improvement or enhancement in instructional practices are essential for creating comprehensive learning communities. In order to promote the vision, mission and action plans of school communities, teachers must be given the toolkits to maximize instructional performances. The development of student-centered learning communities that foster the academic capacities and learning synthesis for all students should be the fundamental goal of professional development for teachers.

The level of professional development may include traditional district workshops that enhance instructional expectations for teachers or the more complicated multiple day workshops given by national and state educational organizations to enhance the federal accountability of skill and professional development for teachers. Most workshops on the national and state level provide clock hours that can be used to renew certifications for teachers every five years. Typically, 150 clock hours is the standard certification number needed to provide a five year certification renewal, so teachers must attend and complete paperwork for a diversity of workshops that range from 1-150 clock hours according to the timeframe of the workshops.

Most districts and schools provide in-service professional development opportunities for teachers during the school year dealing with district objectives/expectations and relevant workshops or classes that can enhance the teaching practices for teachers. Clock hours are provided with each class or workshop and the type of professional development being offered to teachers determines clock hours. Each year, schools are required to report the number of workshops, along with the participants attending the workshops to the Superintendent's office for filing. Teachers collecting clock hour forms are required to file the forms to maintain certification eligibility and job eligibility.

The research by the National Association of Secondary Principals,' "Breaking Ranks II: Strategies for Leading High School Reform" created the following multiple listing of educational practices needed for expanding the professional development opportunities for teachers:

- Interdisciplinary instruction between subject areas
- Identification of individual learning styles to maximize student academic performance
- Training teachers in understanding and applying multiple assessment formats and implementations in curriculum and instruction
- Looking at multiple methods of classroom management strategies
- Providing teachers with national, federal, state and district curriculum expectations and performance outcomes
- Identifying the school communities' action plan of student learning objectives and teacher instructional practices
- Helping teachers understand how to use data to impact student learning goals and objectives
- Teaching teachers on how to disaggregate student data in improving instruction and curriculum implementation for student academic equity and access
- Develop leadership opportunities for teachers to become school and district trainers to promote effective learning communities for student achievement and success

In promoting professional development opportunities for teachers that enhance student achievement, the bottom line is that teachers must be given the time to complete workshops at no or minimal costs. School and district budgets must include financial resources to support and encourage teachers to engage in mandatory and optional professional development opportunities that create a "win-win" learning experience for students.

Whether a teacher is using criterion-referenced, norm-referenced or performance-based data to inform and impact student learning and achievement, the more important objective is ensuring that teachers know how to effectively use the data to improve and reflect upon existing teaching instructions. The goal of identifying ways for teachers to use the school data is simple, "Is the teacher's instructional practice improving student learning goals and academic success?"

School data can include demographic profiling, cultural and ethnic academic trends, state and/or national assessments, portfolios, academic subject pre-post assessment and weekly assessments, projects, and disciplinary reports. By looking at trends and discrepancies in school data, teachers can ascertain whether they are meeting the goals and objectives of the state, national, and federal mandates for school improvement reform and curriculum implementation.

Assessments can be used to motivate students to learn and shape the learning environment to provide learning stimulation that optimizes student access to learning. Butler and McMunn (2006) have shown that "factors that help motivate students to learn are: (1) involving students in their own assessment, (2) matching assessment strategies to student learning, and (3) considering thinking styles and using assessments to adjust the classroom environment in order to enhance student motivation to learn." Teachers can shape the way students learn by creating engaging learning opportunities that promote student achievement.

Skill 11.2   **Recognizes the responsibilities and requirements associated with the development and implementation of Individualized Education Programs (IEPs).**

See Skill 11.3

Skill 11.3   **Demonstrates knowledge of laws related to students' rights in various situations (e.g., in relation to due process, discrimination, harassment, confidentiality, discipline, privacy).**

One of the first things that a teacher learns is how to obtain resources and help for his/her students. All schools have guidelines for receiving this assistance especially since the implementation of the Americans with Disabilities Act. The first step in securing help is for the teacher to approach the school's administration or exceptional education department for direction in attaining special services or resources for qualifying students. Many schools have a committee designated for addressing these needs such as a Child Study Team or Core Team. These teams are made up of both regular and exceptional education teachers, school psychologists, guidance counselors, and administrators. The particular student's classroom teacher usually has to complete some initial paper work and will need to do some behavioral observations.

The teacher will take this information to the appropriate committee for discussion and consideration. The committee will recommend the next step to be taken. Often subsequent steps include a complete psychological evaluation along with certain physical examinations such as vision and hearing screening and a complete medical examination by a doctor.

The referral of students for this process is usually relatively simple for the classroom teacher and requires little more than some initial paper work and discussion. The services and resources the student receives as a result of the process typically prove to be invaluable to the student with learning and/or behavioral disorders.

At times, the teacher must go beyond the school system to meet the needs of some students. An awareness of special services and resources and how to obtain them is essential to all teachers and their students. When the school system is unable to address the needs of a student, the teacher often must take the initiative and contact agencies within the community. Frequently there is no special policy for finding resources. It is simply up to the individual teacher to be creative and resourceful and to find whatever assistance the student needs. Meeting the needs of all students is certainly a team effort that is most often spearheaded by the classroom teacher.

Family involvement

Under the IDEA, parent/guardian involvement in the development of the student's IEP (Individualized Educational Plan) is required and absolutely essential for the advocacy of the disabled student's educational needs. IEPs must be tailored to meet the student's needs, and no one knows those needs better than the parent/guardian and other significant family members. Optimal conditions for a disabled student's education exist when teachers, school administrators, special education professionals and parents/guardians work together to design and execute the IEP.

Due process

Under the IDEA, Congress provides safeguards for students against schools' actions, including the right to sue in court, and encourages states to develop hearing and mediation systems to resolve disputes. No student or their parents/guardians can be denied due process because of disability.

Inclusion, mainstreaming, and least restrictive environment

Inclusion, mainstreaming and least restrictive environment are interrelated policies under the IDEA, with varying degrees of statutory imperatives. Inclusion is the right of students with disabilities to be placed in the regular classroom. Least restrictive environment is the mandate that children be educated to the maximum extent appropriate with their non-disabled peers. Mainstreaming is a policy where disabled students can be placed in the regular classroom, as long as such placement does not interfere with the student's educational plan.

Every teacher in the system must understand the purpose and requirements associated with the development and implementation of Individualized Education Programs (IEPs). Each public school student who receives special education and related services must have an Individualized Education Program (IEP). Each IEP must be designed for one student only, and must be a completely individualized document. The IEP creates an opportunity for teachers, parents, school administrators, related services personnel, and students (when appropriate) to work together to improve educational results for students with disabilities. The IEP is the cornerstone of a quality education for each child with a disability. To create an effective IEP, parents, teachers, other relevant school staff (as identified)--and often the student--must come together to evaluate the student's unique circumstances and the needs that must be addressed. These individuals pool knowledge, experience and commitment to design an educational program (a workable plan) that will enable the student to be involved in, and progress in, the general curriculum. The IEP guides the delivery of special education supports and services for the student with a disability.

Process and Requirements

Step 1. A child is identified as possibly needing special education and related services. The state is required to identify, locate, and evaluate all children with disabilities in the state who need special education and related services. Once identified, parental/legal guardian consent is needed before the child may be evaluated. Evaluation needs to be completed within a reasonable time after consent is granted.

Step 2. The child is evaluated. The evaluation must assess the child in all areas related to the child's suspected disability. The evaluation results will be used to decide the child's eligibility for special education and related services and to make decisions about an appropriate educational program for the child. If the parents/guardians disagree with the evaluation, they have the right to take their child for an Independent Educational Evaluation (IEE). They can ask that the school system pay for this IEE.

Step 3. Eligibility is determined. A group of qualified professionals and the parents/legal guardians review the child's evaluation results. Together, they decide if the child is a "child with a disability," as defined by IDEA.

Step 4. If the child is found eligible for services (in accordance with IDEA), he or she is eligible for special education and related services. Within 30 calendar days after a child is determined eligible, the IEP team must meet to write an IEP for the child.

Step 5. The IEP meeting is scheduled and conducted by appropriate members of the school. School staff must notify all participants and attempt to accommodate parents/guardians and all other participants as to the scheduling for time and location of the meeting.

Step 6. The IEP meeting is held and the IEP is written. Before the school system may provide special education and related services to the child for the first time, the parents/guardians must give consent. The child begins to receive services as soon as possible after the meeting. If the parents/legal guardians do not agree with the IEP and placement, they may discuss their concerns with other members of the IEP team and try to work out an agreement. If they still disagree, they can ask for mediation, or the school may offer mediation. They may file a complaint with the state education agency and may request a due process hearing, at which time mediation must be available.

Step 7. Services are provided. The school system must ensure that the child's IEP is being carried out as it was written. Parents/guardians are given a copy of the IEP. Each of the child's teachers and service providers has access to the IEP and knows his or her specific responsibilities for carrying out the IEP. This includes the accommodations, modifications, and supports that must be provided to the child, in keeping with the IEP.

Step 8. Progress is measured and reported. The child's progress toward the annual goals is measured, as stated in the IEP. His or her parents/guardians are regularly informed of their child's progress and whether that progress is enough for the child to achieve the goals by the end of the year. These progress reports must be provided at least as often as parents/guardians are informed of their non disabled children's progress.

Step 9. The IEP is reviewed. The child's IEP is reviewed by the IEP team at least once a year (more often if the parents/guardians or school officials ask for a review). If necessary, the IEP is revised. Parents/guardians, as team members, must be invited to attend these meetings. Parents can make suggestions for changes, can agree or disagree with the IEP goals, and agree or disagree with the placement. If parents do not agree with the IEP and placement, they may discuss their concerns with other members of the IEP team and try to work out an agreement. There are several options, including additional testing, an independent evaluation, or asking for mediation (if available) or a due process hearing. They may also file a complaint with the state education agency.

Step 10. The child is reevaluated at least every three years. This evaluation is often called a "triennial." Its purpose is to find out if the child continues to be a "child with a disability," as defined by IDEA, and what the child's educational needs are. However, the child must be reevaluated more often if conditions warrant or if the child's parents/guardians or teachers ask for a new evaluation.

Contents of the IEP

By law, the IEP must include certain information about the child and the educational program designed to meet his or her unique needs.

- Current performance.
  The IEP must state how the child is currently performing in school (known as present levels of educational performance). This information usually comes from evaluation results such as classroom tests and assignments, individual tests given to decide eligibility for services or during reevaluation, and observations made by parents, teachers, related service providers, and other school staff. The statement about "current performance" includes how the child's disability affects his or her involvement and progress in the general curriculum.
- Annual goals.
  These are goals that the child can reasonably accomplish in a year. The goals are broken down into short-term objectives or benchmarks. Goals may be academic, social or behavioral, relate to physical needs, or address other educational needs. The goals must be measurable.
- Special education and related services.
  The IEP must list the special education and related services to be provided to the child or on behalf of the child. This includes supplementary aids and services that the child needs. It also includes modifications (changes) to the program or supports for school personnel--such as training or professional development--that will be provided to assist the child.
- Participation with non disabled children. The IEP must explain the extent (if any) to which the child will not participate with non disabled children in the regular class and other school activities.
- Participation in state and district-wide tests.
  The IEP must state what modifications in the administration of these tests the child will need. If a test is not appropriate for the child, the IEP must state why the test is not appropriate and how the child will be tested instead.
- Dates and places.
  The IEP must state when services will begin, how often they will be provided, where they will be provided, and how long they will last.
- Transition service needs.
  Beginning when the child is age 14 (or younger, if appropriate), the IEP must address (within the applicable parts of the IEP) the courses the student needs to take to reach his or her post-school goals. A statement of transition services needs must also be included in each of the child's subsequent IEPs.
- Needed transition services.
  Beginning when the child is age 16 (or younger, if appropriate), the IEP must state what transition services are needed to help the child prepare for leaving school.

- Age of majority.
  Beginning at least one year before the child reaches the age of majority, the IEP must include a statement that the student has been told of any rights that will transfer to him or her at the age of majority (where applicable).
- Measuring progress.
  The IEP must state how the child's progress will be measured and how parents/legal guardians will be informed of that progress.

Abuse Situations

The child who is undergoing the abuse is the one whose needs must be served first. A suspected case gone unreported may destroy a child's life, and their subsequent life as a functional adult. It is the duty of any citizen who suspects abuse and neglect to make a report, and it is especially important and required for State licensed and certified persons to make a report. All reports can be kept confidential if required, but it is best to disclose your identity in case more information is required of you. This is a personal matter that has no impact on qualifications for license or certification. Failure to make a report when abuse or neglect is suspected is punishable by revocation of certification and license, a fine, and criminal charges.

It is the right of any accused individual to have counsel and make a defense, as in any matter of law. The procedure for reporting makes clear the rights of the accused, who stands before the court innocent until proven guilty, with the right to representation, redress and appeal, as in all matters of United States law. The State is cautious about receiving spurious reports, but investigates any that seem real enough.

A teacher is obligated to report suspected abuse immediately. There is no time given as an acceptable or safe period of time to wait before reporting, so hesitation to report may be a cause for action against you. Do not wait once your suspicion is firm. All you need to have is a reasonable suspicion, not actual proof, which is the job for the investigators.

Emotional Difficulties

Many safe and helpful interventions are available to the classroom teacher when dealing with a student who is suffering serious emotional disturbances. First, and foremost, the teacher must maintain open communication with the parents and other professionals who are involved with the student whenever overt behavior characteristics are exhibited. Students with behavior disorders need constant behavior modification, which may involve two-way communication between the home and school on a daily basis.

The teacher must establish an environment that promotes appropriate behavior for all students as well as respect for one another. The students may need to be informed of any special needs that their classmates may have so they can give due consideration. The teacher should also initiate a behavior modification program for any student that might show emotional or behavioral disorders. Such behavior modification plans can be effective means of preventing deviant behavior. If deviant behavior does occur, the teacher should have arranged for a safe and secure time-out place where the student can go for a respite and an opportunity to regain self-control.

Often when a behavior disorder is more severe, the student must be involved in a more concentrated program aimed at alleviating deviant behavior such as psychotherapy. In such instances, the school psychologist, guidance counselor, or behavior specialist is directly involved with the student and provides counseling and therapy on a regular basis. Frequently they are also involved with the student's family.

As a last resort, many families are turning to drug therapy. Once viewed as a radical step, administering drugs to children to balance their emotions or control their behavior has become a widely used form of therapy. Of course, only a medical doctor can prescribe such drugs. Great care must be exercised when giving pills to children in order to change their behavior, especially since so many medicines have undesirable side effects. It is important to know that these drugs relieve only the symptoms of behavior and do not get at the underlying causes. Parents and teachers need to be educated as to the side effects of these medications.

Skill 11.4   Demonstrates knowledge of a teacher's rights and responsibilities in various situations (e.g., in relation to students with disabilities or students who may be abused, speaking out publicly against a school policy).

See Skill 11.3 for information about students with disabilities and students who may be abused.

Speaking out against school policy

A teacher does not want to lose his or her position over a difference of opinion. This is one reason it is key to remain level-headed when dealing with an argumentative person, be it a parent, student, or peer.

Passions—and tempers—tend to run high when people have very definite ideas and feelings about policies. For example, there has been much debate and argument about "zero tolerance" policies which gives strict punishment at the first offense, no matter how small that offense might be. (A "zero tolerance" drug policy, for example, might expel a student if he or she is found with aspirin or ibuprofen.)

Remind an argumentative parent that you did not write the policy they are contesting, but that as a teacher you are bound to uphold that policy. Have the school principal and superintendent advocate on your behalf in this situation. Parents, students, and even other teachers have avenues they can use to affect change in policy, but that avenue does not go directly through you. They should lodge complaints to the appropriate venue, petition the school board or Education Department for changes.

It is usually best to have witnesses to any discussion when there is a difference of opinion so that subsequent recounts do not become "he said, she said" or hearsay. Bringing up such topics during a meeting may be appropriate so that there is a record of the discussion in the minutes. In order to get a fair analysis of whether a teacher's response to an attack by a parent, educator, or student was appropriate, witnesses to that attack will be important.

Skill 11.5 Demonstrates knowledge of parents'/guardians' rights and responsibilities in various situations (e.g., in relation to student records, school attendance).

The student permanent record is a file of the student's cumulative educational history. It contains a profile of the student's academic background as well as the student's behavioral and medical background. Other pertinent individual information contained in the permanent record includes the student's attendance, grade averages, and schools attended. Personal information such as parents' names and addresses, immunization records, child's height and weight, and narrative information about the child's progress and physical and mental well being is an important aspect of the permanent record. All information contained within the permanent record is strictly confidential and is only to be discussed with the student's parents or other involved school personnel.

The purpose of the permanent record is to provide applicable information about the student so that the student's individual educational needs can be met. If any specialized testing has been administered, the results are noted in the permanent record. Any special requirements that the student may have are indicated in the permanent record. Highly personal information, including court orders regarding custody, is filed in the permanent record as is appropriate. The importance and value of the permanent record cannot be underestimated. It offers a comprehensive knowledge of the student.

The current teacher is responsible for maintaining the student's permanent record. All substantive information in regard to testing, academic performance, the student's medical condition, and personal events are placed in the permanent record file. Updated information in regard to the student's grades, attendance, and behavior is added annually. These files are kept in a locked fireproof room or file cabinet and cannot be removed from this room unless the person removing them signs a form acknowledging full responsibility for the safe return of the complete file. Again, only the student's parents (or legal guardians), the teacher or other concerned school personnel may view the contents of the permanent record file.

The permanent record file follows the student as he/she moves through the school system with information being updated along the way. Anytime the student leaves a school, the permanent record is transferred with the student. The permanent record is regarded as legal documentation of a student's educational experience.

The contents of any student records should be indicative of the student's academic aptitude and/or achievement. The information contained should never be in any way derogatory or potentially damaging. It is important to keep in mind that others who view the contents of the records may form an opinion of the student based on the information in the student's record or file. Anyone who places information in a student's record must make every effort to give an accurate reflection of the student's performance while maintaining a neutral position as to the student's potential for future success or failure.

The most essential fact to remember in regard to students' records is that the information within is confidential. Although specific policies may vary from one school or district to another, confidentiality remains constant and universal. Teachers never discuss any student or his/her progress with anyone other than the student's parents or essential school personnel. Confidentiality applies to all student information whether it is a student's spelling test, portfolio, standardized test information, report card, or the contents of the permanent record file.

The significance of the student's records is not to be taken lightly. In many instances, teachers have access to a student's records before she actually meets the student. It is important for the teacher to have helpful information about the student without developing any preconceived biases about the student. Careful regard must be given to all information that is added to a student's file without diluting the potential effectiveness of that information. It is also important to be cognizant of the fact that the primary function of student records is that they are intended to be used as a means of developing a better understanding of the students' needs and to generate a more effective plan for meeting these needs.

Skill 11.6   Demonstrates knowledge of the roles and responsibilities of different components of the education system in Arizona

Successfully acquiring the appropriate degree and achieving certification will qualify a person to become a teacher. But a successful teacher is one who never stops being a student. Every teacher who is open and receptive will, of course, learn from experience: teaching in the classroom; interacting with other faculty members, administrators, parents and other interested members of the community; and from the students, themselves. As in all professions, things are constantly changing in the field of education. Educators, government institutions and many allied or interested segments of society are continually studying objectives, methods and various issues, striving to improve our educational system in comprehensive ways. A teacher who does not avail herself or himself of opportunities for professional growth and development may become anachronistic during her or his own teaching career—continually out of step or lagging behind regarding changing standards, requirements, techniques and objectives being instituted without the teacher's complete understanding or ability to implement these effectively.

Every teacher in the system should be aware of the **Arizona Board of Education Character Education Guidelines:**

Guideline #1

- Encouraging Arizona educators to seek out, research and identify programs which provide materials, background and philosophies that help reach these guidelines and may be suitable to your educational organization.

Guideline #2

- Recognizing that instilling moral, ethical and civic characteristics is an intrinsic part of an Arizona educator's responsibilities.

- Examples of characteristics deemed important to the establishment of moral, ethical and civic foundations may include: integrity; dependability; honesty; fairness; generosity; respectfulness; responsibility; etc.

Guideline #3

- Instilling moral, ethical and civic characteristics in Arizona students can be best achieved through positive support structures at the individual, family, school and community levels.

Examples of positive support structures at the individual, family, school and community levels may include:
• Open and continuous communication between all parties, including the student as deemed necessary;
• Respectful and caring relationships;
• Inclusion of parental involvement in actions impacting the instruction of moral, ethical and civic characteristics; and
• Providing an environment that promotes security, learning, and clear expectations of children/students.

Guideline #4

• Recognizing and sustaining the duties, rights and privileges of our nation and the communities we live in.

Examples of sustaining civic responsibilities may include:
• Volunteering in the community; and
• Exercising personal rights.

Skill 11.7   Identifies legal and ethical guidelines in various educational contexts.

The ethical conduct of an educator has undergone extensive scrutiny in today's classrooms. Teachers are under intense rules and regulations to maintain the highest degree of conduct and professionalism in the classroom. Current court cases have examined ethical violations of teachers engaged in improper communication and abuse with students, along with teachers engaged in drug violations and substance abuse in classrooms. It is imperative that teachers educating today's young people have the highest regard for professionalism and be proper role models for students in and out of the classrooms.

The very nature of the teaching profession—the yearly cycle of doing the same thing over and over again—creates the tendency to fossilize, to quit growing, to become complacent. The teachers who are truly successful are those who have built into their own approach to their jobs and to their lives safeguards against that. They see themselves as constant learners. They believe that learning never ends. They are careful never to teach their classes the same as they did the last time. They build in a tendency to reflect on what is happening to their students under their care or what happened this year as compared to last year.

See also Skill 11.3

Sample Test

Directions: Read each item and select the best response.

1. **When are students more likely to understand complex ideas?**
   (Average Rigor) (Skill 1.1)

   A. If they do outside research before coming to class

   B. Later when they write out the definitions of complex words

   C. When they attend a lecture on the subject

   D. When they are clearly defined by the teacher and are given examples and non-examples of the concept

2. **What developmental patterns should a professional teacher assess to meet the needs of the student?**
   (Average Rigor) (Skill 1.1)

   A. Academic, regional, and family background

   B. Social, physical, academic

   C. Academic, physical, and family background

   D. Physical, family, ethnic background

3. **Students who can solve problems mentally have...**
   (Average Rigor) (Skill 1.1)

   A. Reached maturity

   B. Physically developed

   C. Reached the pre-operational stage of thought

   D. Achieved the ability to manipulate objects symbolically

4. **To maintain the flow of events in the classroom, what should an effective teacher do?**
(Average Rigor) (Skill 1.4)

    A.   Work only in small groups

    B.   Use only whole class activities

    C.   Direct attention to content, rather than focusing the class on misbehavior

    D.   Follow lectures with written assignments

5. **Why is it important for a teacher to pose a question before calling on students to answer?**
(Average Rigor) (Skill 1.4)

    A.   It helps manage student conduct

    B.   It keeps the students as a group focused on the class work

    C.   It allows students time to collaborate

    D.   It gives the teacher time to walk among the students

6. **When developing lessons it is imperative teachers provide equity in pedagogy so…**
(Rigorous) (Skill 1.6)

    A.   Unfair labeling of students will occur

    B.   Student experiences will be positive

    C.   Students will achieve academic success

    D.   All of the above

7. **Which of the following is not a communication issue that is related to diversity within the classroom?**
(Average Rigor) (Skill 1.6)

    A.   Learning disorder

    B.   Sensitive terminology

    C.   Body language

    D.   Discussing differing viewpoints and opinions

8. **How many stages of intellectual development does Piaget define?**
(Easy) (Skill 2.1)

    A.   Two

    B.   Four

    C.   Six

    D.   Eight

9. Who developed the theory of multiple intelligences?
(Easy) (Skill 2.1)

A. Bruner

B. Gardner

C. Kagan

D. Cooper

10. Which description of the role of a teacher is no longer an accurate description?
(Rigorous) (Skill 2.3)

A. Guide on the Side

B. Authoritarian

C. Disciplinarian

D. Sage on the Stage

11. Mrs. Peck wants to justify the use of personalized learning communities to her principal. Which of the following reasons should she use?
(Rigorous) (Skill 3.1)

A. They build multiculturalism

B. They provide a supportive environment to address academic and emotional needs

C. They build relationships between students which promote life long learning

D. They are proactive in their nature

12. Personalized learning communities do which of the following?
(Easy) (Skill 3.1)

A. Increase learning

B. Decrease drop-out rates

C. Decrease unproductive student behavior

D. All of the above

13. **Which statement is an example of specific praise?**
(Easy) (Skill 3.2)

   A. "Jose, you are the only person in class not paying attention"

   B. "William, I thought we agreed that you would turn in all of your homework"

   C. "Raul, you did a good job staying in line. See how it helped us get to music class on time"

   D. "Class, you did a great job cleaning up the art room"

14. **Which of the following can impact the desire of students to learn new material?**
(Easy) (Skill 3.2)

   A. Assessment plans

   B. Lesson plans

   C. Enthusiasm

   D. School community

15. **Mrs. Graham has taken the time to reflect, complete observations, and asked for feedback about the interactions between her and her students from her principal. It is obvious by seeking this information out that Mrs. Graham understands which of the following?**
(Rigorous) (Skill 3.2)

   A. The importance of clear communication with the principal

   B. She needs to analyze her effectiveness of classroom interactions

   C. She is clearly communicating with the principal

   D. She cares about her students

16. No matter what difficulties a student may be experiencing, it is the responsibility of the teacher to...
(Easy) (Skill 3.3)

   A. Find appropriate resources to support the family

   B. Act as a liaison between the family and civil agencies

   C. Ensure all students have equal opportunity for academic success

   D. Allow for academic exceptions

17. Mrs. Potts has noticed an undercurrent in her classroom of an unsettled nature. She is in the middle of her math lesson, but still notices that many of her students seem to be having some sort of difficulty. Mrs. Potts stops class and decides to have a class meeting. She understands that even though her math objectives are important, it is equally important to address whatever is troubling her classroom. What is it Mrs. Potts knows?
(Rigorous) (Skill 3.4)

   A. Discipline is important

   B. Social issues can impact academic learning

   C. Maintaining order is important

   D. Social skills instruction is important

18. The concept of efficient use of time includes which of the following?
(Rigorous) (Skill 3.5)

    A. Daily review, seatwork, and recitation of concepts

    B. Lesson initiation, transition, and comprehension check

    C. Review, test, review

    D. Punctuality, management transition, and wait time avoidance

19. What is one way a teacher can supplement verbal praise?
(Average Rigor) (Skill 4.1)

    A. Help students evaluate their own performance and supply self-reinforcement

    B. Give verbal praise more frequently

    C. Give tangible rewards such as stickers or treats

    D. Have students practice giving verbal praise

20. What is a good strategy for teaching ethnically diverse students?
(Average Rigor) (Skill 4.1)

    A. Don't focus on the students' culture

    B. Expect them to assimilate easily into your classroom

    C. Imitate their speech patterns

    D. Include ethnic studies in the curriculum

21. How can text be modified for low-level ESL students?
(Average Rigor) (Skill 4.1)

    A. Add visuals and illustrations

    B. Let students write definitions

    C. Change text to a narrative form

    D. Have students write details out from the text

22. **What is a roadblock to second language learning?** *(Rigorous) (Skill 4.1)*

    A. Students are forced to speak

    B. Students speak only when ready

    C. Mistakes are considered a part of learning

    D. The focus is on oral communication

23. **Students who are learning English as a second language often require which of the following to process new information?** *(Rigorous) (Skill 4.1)*

    A. Translators

    B. Reading tutors

    C. Instruction in their native language

    D. Additional time and repetitions

24. **Many of the current ESL approaches used in classrooms today are based on which approach?** *(Easy) (Skill 4.1)*

    A. Social Learning Methods

    B. Native Tongue Methods

    C. ESL Learning Methods

    D. Special Education Methods

25. **In successful inclusion of students with disabilities:** *(Average Rigor) (Skill 3.4)*

    A. A variety of instructional arrangements are available

    B. School personnel shift the responsibility for learning outcomes to the student

    C. The physical facilities are used as they are

    D. Regular classroom teachers have sole responsibility for evaluating student progress

26. Mr. Weiss understands that it is imperative that students who are struggling with acquiring concepts at a specific grade level can still benefit from participating in whole classroom discussions and lessons. In fact, such students should be required to be present for whole classroom lessons. Mr. Weiss's beliefs fall under which of the following principles?
(Rigorous) (Skill 6.5)

A. Self-fulfilling prophecy

B. Partial participation

C. Inclusion

D. Heterogeneous grouping

27. When is utilization of instructional materials most effective?
(Average Rigorous) (Skill 5.1)

A. When the activities are sequenced

B. When the materials are prepared ahead of time

C. When the students choose the pages to work on

D. When the students create the instructional materials

28. What should a teacher do when students have not responded well to an instructional activity?
(Average Rigor) (Skill 5.1)

A. Reevaluate learner needs

B. Request administrative help

C. Continue with the activity another day

D. Assign homework on the concept

29. Curriculum mapping is an effective strategy because it...
(Rigorous) (Skill 5.1)

A. Provides an orderly sequence to instruction

B. Provides lesson plans for teachers to use and follow

C. Ties the curriculum into instruction

D. Provides a clear map so all students receive the same instruction across all classes

30. **Which of the following is the correct term for the alignment of the curriculum across all grades K-12?**
(Rigorous) (Skill 5.1)

   A. Data Based Decision Making

   B. Curriculum Mapping

   C. Vertical Integration

   D. Curriculum Alignment

31. **When creating and selecting materials for instruction, teachers should complete which of the following steps:**
(Average Rigor) (Skill 5.1)

   A. Make learning relevant to the prior knowledge of the students

   B. Allow for a variation of learning styles

   C. Choose alternative teaching strategies

   D. All of the above

32. **When considering the development of the curriculum, which of the following accurately describes the four factors which need to be considered?**
(Rigorous) (Skill 5.1)

   A. Alignment, Scope, Sequence, and Design

   B. Assessment, Instruction, Design, and Sequence

   C. Data, Alignment, Correlation, and Score

   D. Alignment, Sequence, Design and Assessment

33. **What should be considered when evaluating textbooks for content?**
(Average Rigor) (Skill 5.3)

   A. Type of print used

   B. Number of photos used

   C. Free of cultural stereotyping

   D. Outlines at the beginning of each chapter

34. **What are critical elements of instructional process?** *(Average Rigor) (Skill 5.4)*

    A.   Content, goals, teacher needs

    B.   Means of getting money to regulate instruction

    C.   Content, materials, activities, goals, learner needs

    D.   Materials, definitions, assignments

35. **What would improve planning for instruction?** *(Average Rigor) (Skill 5.4)*

    A.   Describe the role of the teacher and student

    B.   Evaluate the outcomes of instruction

    C.   Rearrange the order of activities

    D.   Give outside assignments

36. **The teacher states that the lesson the students will be engaged in will consist of a review of the material from the previous day, demonstration of the scientific of an electronic circuit, and small group work on setting up an electronic circuit. What has the teacher demonstrated?** *(Rigorous) (Skill 5.4)*

    A.   The importance of reviewing

    B.   Giving the general framework for the lesson to facilitate learning

    C.   Giving students the opportunity to leave if they are not interested in the lesson

    D.   Providing momentum for the lesson

37. Which of the following describes why it is important and necessary for teachers to be able to analyze data on their students?
(Rigorous) (Skill 5.4)

    A.   To provide appropriate instruction

    B.   To make instructional decisions

    C.   To communicate and determine instructional progress

    D.   All of the above

38. The teacher states, "We will work on the first page of vocabulary words. On the second page we will work on the structure and meaning of the words. We will go over these together and then you will write out the answers to the exercises on your own. I will be circulating to give help if needed". What is this an example of?
(Rigorous) (Skill 5.4)

    A.   Evaluation of instructional activity

    B.   Analysis of instructional activity

    C.   Identification of expected outcomes

    D.   Pacing of instructional activity

39. If teachers attend to content, instructional materials, activities, learner needs, and goals in instructional planning, what could be an outcome?
(Rigorous) (Skill 5.4)

    A.   Planning for the next year

    B.   Effective classroom performance

    C.   Elevated test scores on standardized tests

    D.   More student involvement

40. What is one component of the instructional planning model that must be given careful evaluation?
(Rigorous) (Skill 5.5)

    A.   Students' prior knowledge and skills

    B.   The script the teacher will use in instruction

    C.   Future lesson plans

    D.   Parent participation

41. **What steps are important in the review of subject matter in the classroom?**
(Rigorous) (Skill 5.5)

    A. A lesson-initiating review, topic and a lesson-end review

    B. A preview of the subject matter, an in-depth discussion, and a lesson-end review

    C. A rehearsal of the subject matter and a topic summary within the lesson

    D. A short paragraph synopsis of the previous day's lesson and a written review at the end of the lesson

42. **Which of the following is true about "readiness to learn?"**
(Rigorous) (Skill 5.5)

    A. It is possible to assess each student's readiness for each lesson.

    B. The concept of readiness is a not a developmentally based phenomenon.

    C. Readiness for subject area learning is also dependent on factors such as interest, motivation and attitude.

    D. None of the above.

43. **When planning instruction, which of the following is an organizational tool to help ensure you are providing a well balanced set of objectives?**
(Rigorous) (Skill 5.5)

    A. Using taxonomy to develop objectives

    B. Determining prior knowledge skill levels

    C. Determining readiness levels

    D. Ensuring you meet the needs of diverse learners

44. Mr. Garcia is a math coach within his building. He is the only math coach in his building and in fact within his district. Mr. Garcia believes it is imperative he seek out the support of colleagues to work in a more collaborative manner. Which of the following would be an appropriate step for him to take?
(Rigorous) (Skill 5.7)

A. Collaborating with other teachers in his building regardless of their skill level knowledge in his area

B. Asking for the administration to find colleagues with which he can collaborate

C. Joining a professional organization such as the NCTM

D. Searching the internet for possible collaboration opportunities

45. In the past, teaching has been viewed as _____ while in more current society it has been viewed as _____.
(Rigorous) (Skill 5.7)

A. Isolating....collaborative

B. Collaborative....isolating

C. Supportive.....isolating

D. Isolating.... Supportive

46. How are standardized tests useful in assessment?
(Average Rigor) (Skill 6.1)

A. For teacher evaluation

B. For evaluation of the administration

C. For comparison from school to school

D. For comparison to the population on which the test was normed

47. Which of the following is NOT used in evaluating test items?
(Rigorous) (Skill 6.1)

A. Student feedback

B. Content validity

C. Reliability

D. Ineffective coefficient

48. **How will students have a fair chance to demonstrate what they know on a test?**
(Average Rigor) (Skill 6.2)

A. The examiner has strictly enforced rules for taking the test

B. The examiner provides a comfortable setting free of distractions and positively encourages the students

C. The examiner provides frequent stretch breaks to the students

D. The examiner stresses the importance of the test to the overall grade

49. **What is an example of formative feedback?**
(Average Rigor) (Skill 6.2)

A. The results of an intelligence test

B. Correcting the tests in small groups

C. Verbal behavior that expresses approval of a student response to a test item

D. Scheduling a discussion prior to the test

50. **What does the validity of a test refer to?**
(Easy) (Skill 6.2)

A. Its consistency

B. Its usefulness

C. Its accuracy

D. The degree of true scores it provides

51. **Safeguards against bias and discrimination in the assessment of children include:**
(Average Rigor) (Skill 6.2)

A. The testing of a child in standard English

B. The requirement for the use of one standardized test

C. The use of evaluative materials in the child's native language or other mode of communication

D. All testing performed by a certified, licensed, psychologist

52. **When a teacher wants to utilize an assessment which is subjective in nature, which of the following is the most effective method for scoring?**
(Easy) (Skill 4.6)

   A. Rubric

   B. Checklist

   C. Alternative Assessment

   D. Subjective measures should not be utilized

53. **What is an effective way to prepare students for testing?**
(Average Rigor) (Skill 6.4)

   A. Minimize the importance of the test

   B. Orient the students to the test, telling them of the purpose, how the results will be used and how it is relevant to them

   C. Use the same format for every test are given

   D. Have them construct an outline to study from

54. **Discovery learning is to inquiry as direct instruction is to...**
(Rigorous) (Skill 7.1)

   A. Scripted lessons

   B. Well-developed instructions

   C. Clear instructions which eliminate all misinterpretations

   D. Creativity of teaching

55. **What do cooperative learning methods all have in common?**
(Average Rigor) (Skill 7.1)

   A. Philosophy

   B. Cooperative task/cooperative reward structures

   C. Student roles and communication

   D. Teacher roles

56. The use of technology in the classroom allows for... *(Easy) (Skill 7.1)*

   A. More complex lessons

   B. Better delivery of instruction

   C. Variety of instruction

   D. Better ability to meet more individual student needs

57. When asking questions of students it is important to... *(Easy) (Skill 7.3)*

   A. Use questions the students can answer

   B. Provide numerous questions

   C. Provide questions at various levels

   D. Provide only a limited about of questions

58. Which of following is <u>not</u> the role of the teacher in the instructional process? *(Average Rigor) (Skill 7.5)*

   A. Instructor

   B. Coach

   C. Facilitator

   D. Follower

59. What do cooperative learning methods all have in common? *(Average Rigor) (Skill 7.6)*

   A. Philosophy

   B. Cooperative task/cooperative reward structures

   C. Student roles and communication

   D. Teacher roles

60. Which of the following is an accurate description of ESL students? *(Easy) (Skill 8.5)*

   A. Remedial students

   B. Exceptional education students

   C. Are not a homogeneous group

   D. Feel confident in communicating in English when with their peers

61. **What is an effective way to help a non-English speaking student succeed in class?**
(Rigorous) (Skill 8.5)

   A.   Refer the child to a specialist

   B.   Maintain an encouraging, success-oriented atmosphere

   C.   Help them assimilate by making them use English exclusively

   D.   Help them cope with the content materials you presently use

62. **Mrs. Grant is providing her students with many extrinsic motivators in order to increase their intrinsic motivation. Which of the following best explains this relationship?**
(Rigorous) (Skill 9.2)

   A.   This is a good relationship and will increase intrinsic motivation

   B.   The relationship builds animosity between the teacher and the students

   C.   Extrinsic motivation does not in itself help to build intrinsic motivation

   D.   There is no place for extrinsic motivation in the classroom

63. **What has been established to increase student originality, intrinsic motivation, and higher order thinking skills?**
(Rigorous) (Skill 9.2)

   A.   Classroom climate

   B.   High expectations

   C.   Student choice

   D.   Use of authentic learning opportunities

64. **How can the teacher establish a positive climate in the classroom?**
(Average Rigor) (Skill 9.4)

    A.   Help students see the unique contributions of individual differences

    B.   Use whole group instruction for all content areas

    C.   Help students divide into cooperative groups based on ability

    D.   Eliminate teaching strategies that allow students to make choices

65. **How can student misconduct be redirected at times?**
(Average Rigor) (Skill 9.5)

    A.   The teacher threatens the students

    B.   The teacher assigns detention to the whole class

    C.   The teacher stops the activity and stares at the students

    D.   The teacher effectively handles changing from one activity to another

66. **What is one way of effectively managing student conduct?**
(Average Rigor) (Skill 9.6)

    A.   State expectations about behavior

    B.   Let students discipline their peers

    C.   Let minor infractions of the rules go unnoticed

    D.   Increase disapproving remarks

67. **What is a sample of an academic transition signal?**
(Average Rigor) (Skill 9.6)

    A.   "How do clouds form?"

    B.   "Today we are going to study clouds."

    C.   "We have completed today's lesson."

    D.   "That completes the description of cumulus clouds. Now we will look at the description of cirrus clouds."

68. A parent has left an angry message on the teacher's voicemail. The message relates to a concern about a student and is directed at the teacher. The teacher should:
(Average Rigor) (Skill 10.1)

   A. Call back immediately and confront the parent

   B. Cool off, plan what to discuss with the parent, then call back

   C. Question the child to find out what set off the parent

   D. Ignore the message,

69. Mr. Brown wishes to improve his parent communication skills. Which of the following is a strategy he can utilize to accomplish this goal?
(Easy) (Skill 10.1)

   A. Hold parent-teacher conferences

   B. Send home positive notes

   C. Have parent nights where the parents are invited into his classroom

   D. All of the above

70. Tommy is a student in your class, his parents are deaf. Tommy is struggling with math and you want to contact the parents to discuss the issues. How should you proceed?
(Easy) (Skill 10.1)

   A. Limit contact due to the parent's inability to hear

   B. Use a TTY phone to communicate with the parents

   C. Talk to your administrator to find an appropriate interpreter to help you communicate with the parents personally

   D. Both B and C but not A

71. When communicating with parents for whom English is not the primary language you should:
(Easy) (Skill 10.1)

   A. Provide materials whenever possible in their native language

   B. Use an interpreter

   C. Provide the same communication as you would to native English speaking parents

   D. All of the above

72. Marco's mother is quite irate. She calls in and leaves a message on your voicemail. After listening to the voicemail, which of the following is the most appropriate response for you to make?
(Easy) (Skill 10.1)

A. Have the principal return the call

B. Ask Marco's mother to come into school for a meeting

C. Ignore the phone call

D. Return the call and discuss the issue over the phone

73. Which of the following is NOT a sound educational practice for expanding the professional development opportunities for teachers?
(Rigorous) (Skill 11.1)

A. Looking at multiple methods of classroom management strategies

B. Training teachers in understanding and applying multiple assessment formats and implementations in curriculum and instruction

C. Having the students complete professional development assessments on a regular basis

D. Teaching teachers how to disaggregate student data in improving instruction and curriculum implementation for student academic equity and access

74. **What would happen if a school utilized an integrated approach to professional development?**
(Rigorous) (Skill 11.1)

   A. All stake holders' needs are addressed

   B. Teachers and administrators are on the same page

   C. High quality programs for students are developed

   D. Parents drive the curriculum and instruction

75. **The child study team is the first line of defense for a teacher when...**
(Rigorous) (Skill 11.3)

   A. A student is in special education

   B. A student is struggling within the regular curriculum

   C. A principal feels a teacher needs support in delivering instruction

   D. A student needs services outside of the school district

76. **A 16 year-old girl who has been looking sad writes an essay in which the main protagonist commits suicide. You overhear her talking about suicide. What do you do?**
(Average Rigor) (Skill 11.3)

   A. Report this immediately to school administration, talk to the girl, letting her know you will talk to her parents about it

   B. Report this immediately to authorities

   C. Report this immediately to school administration. Make your own report to authorities if required by protocol in your school. Do nothing else

   D. Just give the child some extra attention, as it may just be that's all she's looking for

77. Sandy, a student with identified special needs, requires a change in her educational placement. Sandy's parents do not agree with the school system on what is the best educational placement for Sandy. Which of the following is one possible course of action the school system can take?
(Rigorous) (Skill 11.3)

A. Due Process

B. Hold an IEP team meeting

C. Ignore the parent's wishes

D. File suit against the parents

78. Which of the following could be an example of a situation which could have an effect on a student's learning and academic progress?
(Average Rigor) (Skill 11.3)

A. Relocation

B. Abuse

C. Both of the above

D. Neither of the above

79. You receive a phone call from a person who indicates she is now tutoring a student in your class. She would like you to provide an overview of the academic areas which the student is having difficulties. What is the first thing you should do?
(Rigorous) (Skill 11.5)

A. Find a time and talk with the tutor about issues you see within the classroom

B. Call the parents

C. Put together a packet of information to share with the tutor

D. Offer to invite the tutor in to have a discussion and observe the child

80. The IEP should contain all of the following except...

(Average Rigor) (Skill 11.3)

A. Grades

B. Transition Plans

C. Current Performance

D. Service

Answer Key:

1. D	28. A	55. B
2. B	29. A	56. D
3. D	30. C	57. C
4. C	31. D	58. D
5. B	32. A	59. B
6. D	33. C	60. C
7. A	34. C	61. B
8. B	35. B	62. C
9. B	36. B	63. C
10. D	37. D	64. A
11. B	38. B	65. D
12. D	39. B	66. A
13. C	40. A	67. D
14. C	41. A	68. B
15. B	42. C	69. D
16. C	43. A	70. D
17. B	44. C	71. D
18. D	45. A	72. B
19. A	46. D	73. C
20. D	47. D	74. C
21. A	48. B	75. B
22. A	49. C	76. C
23. D	50. B	77. B
24. A	51. C	78. C
25. A	52. A	79. B
26. B	53. B	80. A
27. A	54. C	

Rigor Table

	Easy %20	Average Rigor %40	Rigorous %40
Question #	8,9, 12, 13, 16, 24, 50, 52, 56, 57, 60, 69, 70, 71, 72	1, 2, 3, 4, 5, 7, 19, 20, 21, 25, 27, 28, 31, 33, 34, 35, 46, 48, 49, 51, 53, 55, 58, 59, 64, 65, 66, 67, 68, 76, 78, 80	6, 10, 11, 15, 17, 18, 22, 23, 26, 29, 30, 32, 36, 37, 38, 39, 40, 41, 42, 43, 44, 45, 47, 54, 61, 62, 63, 73, 74, 75, 77, 79

Rationales for Sample Questions

1.   **When are students more likely to understand complex ideas?**
      (Average Rigor) (Skill 1.1)

      A.   If they do outside research before coming to class

      B.   Later when they write out the definitions of complex words

      C.   When they attend a lecture on the subject

      D.   When they are clearly defined by the teacher and are given
            examples and non-examples of the concept

Answer: D. When they are clearly defined by the teacher and are given examples and nonexamples of the concept.

Several studies have been carried out to determine the effectiveness of giving examples as well as the difference in effectiveness of various types of examples. It was found conclusively that the most effective method of concept presentation included giving a definition along with examples and non-examples and also providing an explanation of them. These same studies indicate that boring examples were just as effective as interesting examples in promoting learning. Additional studies have been conducted to determine the most effective number of examples that will result in maximum student learning. These studies concluded that a few thoughtfully selected examples are just as effective as many examples. It was determined that the actual number of examples necessary to promote student learning was relative to the learning characteristics of the learners. It was again ascertained that learning is facilitated when examples are provided along with the definition.

2.   **What developmental patterns should a professional teacher assess to meet the needs of the student?**
     (Average Rigor) (Skill 1.1)

     A.   Academic, regional, and family background

     B.   Social, physical, academic

     C.   Academic, physical, and   family background

     D.   Physical, family, ethnic background

Answer: B. Social, physical, academic.

The effective teacher applies knowledge of physical, social, and academic developmental patterns and of individual differences, to meet the instructional needs of all students in the classroom and. The most important premise of child development is that all domains of development (physical, social, and academic) are integrated. The teacher has a broad knowledge and thorough understanding of the development that typically occurs during the students' current period of life. More importantly, the teacher understands how children learn best during each period of development. An examination of the student's file coupled with ongoing evaluation assures a successful educational experience for both teacher and students.

3.   **Students who can solve problems mentally have...**
     (Average Rigor) (Skill 1.1)

     A.   Reached maturity

     B.   Physically developed

     C.   Reached the pre-operational stage of thought

     D.   Achieved the ability to manipulate objects symbolically

Answer: D. Achieved the ability to manipulate objects symbolically

When students are able to solve mental problems, it is an indication to the teacher that they have achieved the ability to manipulate objects symbolically and should be instructed to continue to develop their cognitive and academic skills.

4. **To maintain the flow of events in the classroom, what should an effective teacher do?**
   (Average Rigor) (Skill 1.4)

   A. Work only in small groups

   B. Use only whole class activities

   C. Direct attention to content, rather than focusing the class on misbehavior

   D. Follow lectures with written assignments

Answer: C. Direct attention to content, rather than focusing the class on misbehavior.

Students who misbehave often do so to attract attention. By focusing the attention of the misbehaver as well as the rest of the class on the real purpose of the classroom sends the message that misbehaving will not be rewarded with class attention to the misbehaver. Engaging students in content by using the various tools available to the creative teacher goes a long way in ensuring a peaceful classroom.

5. **Why is it important for a teacher to pose a question before calling on students to answer?**
   (Average Rigor) (Skill 1.4)

   A. It helps manage student conduct

   B. It keeps the students as a group focused on the class work

   C. It allows students time to collaborate

   D. It gives the teacher time to walk among the students

Answer: B. It keeps the students as a group focused on the class work.

It doesn't take much distraction for a class's attention to become diffused. Once this happens, effectively teaching a principle or a skill is very difficult. The teacher should plan presentations that will keep students focused on the lesson. A very useful tool is effective, well-thought-out, pointed questions.

6.   **When developing lessons it is imperative teachers provide equity in pedagogy so...**
       (Rigorous) (Skill 1.6)

     A.   Unfair labeling of students will occur

     B.   Student experiences will be positive

     C.   Students will achieve academic success

     D.   All of the above

Answer: D. All of the above

Providing equity of pedagogy allows for students to have positive learning experiences, achieve academic success, and helps to prevent the labeling of students in an unfair manner.

7.   **Which of the following is not a communication issue that is related to diversity within the classroom?**
       (Average Rigor) (Skill 1.6)

     A.   Learning disorder

     B.   Sensitive terminology

     C.   Body language

     D.   Discussing differing viewpoints and opinions

Answer: A. Learning disorders

Learning disorders, while they may have a foundation in the specific communication skills of a student, are not in and of themselves a communication issue related to diversity within the classroom.

8. **How many stages of intellectual development does Piaget define?**
   (Easy) (Skill 2.1)

   A. Two

   B. Four

   C. Six

   D. Eight

Answer: B. Four.

The stages are:
1. Sensorimotor stage: from birth to age 2 years (children experience the world through movement and senses).
2. Preoperational stage: from ages 2 to 7(acquisition of motor skills).
3. Concrete operational stage: from ages 7 to 11 (children begin to think logically about concrete events).
4. Formal Operational stage: after age 11 (development of abstract reasoning).

9. **Who developed the theory of multiple intelligences?**
   (Easy) (Skill 2.1)

   A. Bruner

   B. Gardner

   C. Kagan

   D. Cooper

Answer: B. Gardner.

Howard Gardner's most famous work is probably Frames of Mind, which details seven dimensions of intelligence (Visual/Spatial Intelligence, Musical Intelligence, Verbal Intelligence, Logical/Mathematical Intelligence, Interpersonal Intelligence, Intrapersonal Intelligence, and Bodily/Kinesthetic Intelligence). Gardner's claim that pencil and paper IQ tests do not capture the full range of human intelligences has garnered much praise within the field of education but has also met criticism, largely from psychometricians. Since the publication of Frames of Mind, Gardner has additionally identified the 8th dimension of intelligence: Naturalist Intelligence, and is still considering a possible ninth— Existentialist Intelligence.

10.   **Which description of the role of a teacher is no longer an accurate description?**
      (Rigorous) (Skill 2.3)

      A.   Guide on the Side

      B.   Authoritarian

      C.   Disciplinarian

      D.   Sage on the Stage

Answer: D. Sage on the stage

The old phrase of describing a teacher as a sage on the stage is no longer accurate. It is not the responsibility of the teacher to impart his/her knowledge on students. Teachers do not, nor should it be thought that they have all of the answers. In contrast, it is the responsibility of the teacher to guide students through the learning process.

11.   **Mrs. Peck wants to justify the use of personalized learning communities to her principal. Which of the following reasons should she use?**
      (Rigorous) (Skill 3.1)

      A.   They build multiculturalism

      B.   They provide a supportive environment to address academic and emotional needs

      C.   They build relationships between students which promote life long learning

      D.   They are proactive in their nature

Answer: B. They provide a supportive environment to address academic and emotional needs

While professional learning communities do all of the choices provided, this question asks for a justification statement. The best justification of those choices provided for implementing a personalized learning community in a classroom is to provide a supportive environment to help address the academic and emotional needs of her students.

12.   **Personalized learning communities do which of the following?**
       (Easy) (Skill 3.1)

      A.   Increase learning

      B.   Decrease drop-out rates

      C.   Decrease unproductive student behavior

      D.   All of the above

Answer: D. All of the above

Researchers show that personalized learning environments increase the learning affect for students, decrease drop-out rates among marginalized students, and decrease unproductive student behavior that can result from constant cultural misunderstandings or miscues between students.

13.   **Which statement is an example of specific praise?**
       (Easy) (Skill 3.2)

      A.   "Jose, you are the only person in class not paying attention"

      B.   "William, I thought we agreed that you would turn in all of your homework"

      C.   "Raul, you did a good job staying in line. See how it helped us get to music class on time"

      D.   "Class, you did a great job cleaning up the art room"

Answer: C. "Raul, you did a good job staying in line. See how it helped us get to music class on time?"

Praise is a powerful tool in obtaining and maintaining order in a classroom. In addition, it is an effective motivator. It is even more effective if the positive results of good behavior are included.

14. **Which of the following can impact the desire of students to learn new material?**
    (Easy) (Skill 3.2)

    A.   Assessment plans

    B.   Lesson plans

    C.   Enthusiasm

    D.   School community

Answer: C. Enthusiasm

The enthusiasm a teacher exhibits can not only have positive effects on students' desire to learn, but also on on-task behaviors as well.

15. **Mrs. Graham has taken the time to reflect, complete observations, and asked for feedback about the interactions between her and her students from her principal. It is obvious by seeking this information out that Mrs. Graham understands which of the following?**
    (Rigorous) (Skill 3.2)

    A.   The importance of clear communication with the principal

    B.   She needs to analyze her effectiveness of classroom interactions

    C.   She is clearly communicating with the principal

    D.   She cares about her students

Answer: B. She needs to analyze her effectiveness of classroom interactions

Utilizing reflection, observations and feedback from peers or supervisors, teachers can help to build their own understanding of how they interact with students. In this way, they can better analyze their effectiveness at building appropriate relationships with students.

16. **No matter what difficulties a student may be experiencing, it is the responsibility of the teacher to…**
(Easy) (Skill 3.3)

    A.   Find appropriate resources to support the family

    B.   Act as a liaison between the family and civil agencies

    C.   Ensure all students have equal opportunity for academic success

    D.   Allow for academic exceptions

Answer: C. Ensure all students have equal opportunity for academic success

Regardless of the positive or negative impacts on the students' education from outside sources, it is the teacher's responsibility to ensure that all students in the classroom have an equal opportunity for academic success. This begins with the teacher's statement of high expectations for every student, and develops through planning, delivery and evaluation of instruction which provides for inclusion and ensures that all students have equal access to the resources necessary for successful acquisition of the academic skills being taught and measured in the classroom.

17.   Mrs. Potts has noticed an undercurrent in her classroom of an unsettled nature. She is in the middle of her math lesson, but still notices that many of her students seem to be having some sort of difficulty. Mrs. Potts stops class and decides to have a class meeting.   She understands that even though her math objectives are important, it is equally important to address whatever is troubling her classroom. What is it Mrs. Potts knows?
(Rigorous) (Skill 3.4)

   A.   Discipline is important

   B.   Social issues can impact academic learning

   C.   Maintaining order is important

   D.   Social skills instruction is important

Answer: B. Social issues can impact academic learning

Mrs. Potts understands that as long as there is a social situation or issue in the classroom, it is unlikely that any academics she presents will be learned. All of those areas instructed are important; however, it is this understanding of the fact that the academics will be impacted that is important in this particular situation as she is interrupting her math instruction.

18.   The concept of efficient use of time includes which of the following?
(Rigorous) (Skill 3.5)

   A.   Daily review, seatwork, and recitation of concepts

   B.   Lesson initiation, transition, and comprehension check

   C.   Review, test, review

   D.   Punctuality, management transition, and wait time avoidance

Answer: D. Punctuality, management transition, and wait time avoidance.

One who succeeds in managing a business follows these rules; so does the successful teacher.

19. **What is one way a teacher can supplement verbal praise?**
    (Average Rigor) (Skill 4.1)

    A.   Help students evaluate their own performance and supply self-reinforcement

    B.   Give verbal praise more frequently

    C.   Give tangible rewards such as stickers or treats

    D.   Have students practice giving verbal praise

Answer: A. Help students evaluate their own performance and supply self-reinforcement.

While praise is useful in maintaining order in a classroom and in motivating students, it's important for the teacher to remember at all times that one major educational objective is that of preparing students to succeed in the world once the supports of the classroom are gone. Self-esteem (or lack of it) is often barriers to success. An important lesson and skill for students to learn is how to bolster one's own self-esteem and confidence.

20. **What is a good strategy for teaching ethnically diverse students?**
    (Average Rigor) (Skill 4.1)

    A.   Don't focus on the students' culture

    B.   Expect them to assimilate easily into your classroom

    C.   Imitate their speech patterns

    D.   Include ethnic studies in the curriculum

Answer: D. Include ethnic studies in the curriculum.

Exploring students' own cultures increases their confidence levels in the group. It is also a very useful tool when students are struggling to develop identities that they can feel comfortable with. The bonus is that this is good training for living in the world.

21. **How can text be modified for low-level ESL students?**
    (Average Rigor) (Skill 4.1)

    A.   Add visuals and illustrations

    B.   Let students write definitions

    C.   Change text to a narrative form

    D.   Have students write details out from the text

Answer: A. Add visuals and illustrations.

No matter what name we put on it, a book is a book. If students can see the object, not only will they be able to compare their own word for it, a useful tool in learning a new language, but the object can serve as a mnemonic device. The teacher might use actual objects in a classroom to facilitate learning the new language.

22. **What is a roadblock to second language learning?**
    (Rigorous) (Skill 4.1)

    A.   Students are forced to speak.

    B.   Students speak only when ready.

    C.   Mistakes are considered a part of learning.

    D.   The focus is on oral communication.

Answer: A. Students are forced to speak.
It's embarrassing for anyone who is in a foreign-language environment to be forced to expose his inability to use that language before he is ready. Being flexible with these students until they're ready to try their wings will shorten the time it will take to approach fluency.

23. **Students who are learning English as a second language often require which of the following to process new information?**
    (Rigorous) (Skill 4.1)

    A.   Translators

    B.   Reading tutors

    C.   Instruction in their native language

    D.   Additional time and repetitions

Answer: D. Additional time and repetitions

While there are varying thoughts and theories into the most appropriate instruction for ESL students, much ground can be gained by simply providing additional repetitions and time for new concepts. It is important to include visuals and the other senses into every aspect of this instruction.

24. **Many of the current ESL approaches used in classrooms today are based on which approach?**
    (Easy) (Skill 4.1)

    A.   Social Learning Methods

    B.   Native Tongue Methods

    C.   ESL Learning Methods

    D.   Special Education Methods

Answer. A. Social Learning Methods

Placing students in mixed groups and pairing them with native speakers, ESL students are given the opportunities to practice English in a more natural setting.

25. In successful inclusion of students with disabilities:
(Average Rigor) (Skill 3.4)

A. A variety of instructional arrangements are available

B. School personnel shift the responsibility for learning outcomes to the student

C. The physical facilities are used as they are

D. Regular classroom teachers have sole responsibility for evaluating student progress

Answer: A. A variety of instructional arrangements are available

Here are some support systems and activities that are in evidence where successful inclusion has occurred:

Attitudes and beliefs
- the regular teacher believes the student can succeed.
- school personnel are committed to accepting responsibility for the learning outcomes of students with disabilities.
- school personnel and the students in the class have been prepared to receive a student with disabilities

Services and Physical accommodations
- services needed by the student are available (e.g. health, physical, occupational, or speech therapy).
- accommodations to the physical plant and equipment are adequate to meet the students' needs (e.g. toys, building and playground facilities, learning materials, assistive devices).

School support
- the principal understands the needs of students with disabilities
- adequate numbers of personnel, including aides and support personnel, are available
- adequate staff development and technical assistance, based on the needs of the school personnel, are being provided (e.g. information on disabilities, instructional methods, awareness and acceptance activities for students and team-building skills).
- appropriate policies and procedures for monitoring individual student progress, including grading and testing are in place

Collaboration

- special educators are part of the instructional or planning team
- teaming approaches are used for program implementation and problem solving
- regular teachers, special education teachers, and other specialists collaborate (e.g. co-teach, team teach, work together on teacher assistance teams).

Instructional methods

- teachers have the knowledge and skills needed to select and adapt curricular and instructional methods according to individual student needs
- a variety of instructional arrangements is available (e.g. team teaching, cross-grade grouping, peer tutoring, and teacher assistance teams). teachers foster a cooperative learning environment and promote socialization.

26. **Mr. Weiss understands that it is imperative that students who are struggling with acquiring concepts at a specific grade level can still benefit from participating in whole classroom discussions and lessons. In fact, such students should be required to be present for whole classroom lessons. Mr. Weiss's beliefs fall under which of the following principles?**
(Rigorous) (Skill 6.5)

A. Self-fulfilling prophecy

B. Partial participation

C. Inclusion

D. Heterogeneous grouping

Answer: B. Partial participation

The concept of partial participation indicates that children, even those struggling, can participate in complex concepts at least to a partial degree. While they may not be able to complete all of the requirements of a lesson objective, they may be able complete portions of the objective and will benefit from that additional learning in a positive manner.

27. **When is utilization of instructional materials most effective?**
    (Average Rigorous) (Skill 5.1)

    A.   When the activities are sequenced

    B.   When the materials are prepared ahead of time

    C.   When the students choose the pages to work on

    D.   When the students create the instructional materials

Answer: A. When the activities are sequenced.

Most assignments will require more than one educational principle. It is helpful to explain to students the proper order in which these principles must be applied to complete the assignment successfully. Subsequently, students should also be informed of the nature of the assignment (i.e., cooperative learning, group project, individual assignment, etc). This is often done at the start of the assignment.

28. **What should a teacher do when students have not responded well to an instructional activity?**
(Average Rigor) (Skill 5.1)

    A.   Reevaluate learner needs

    B.   Request administrative help

    C.   Continue with the activity another day

    D.   Assign homework on the concept

Answer: A. Reevaluate learner needs.

The value of teacher observations cannot be underestimated. It is through the use of observations that the teacher is able to informally assess the needs of the students during instruction. These observations will drive the lesson and determine the direction that the lesson will take based on student activity and behavior. After a lesson is carefully planned, teacher observation is the single most important component of an instructional presentation. If the teacher observes that a particular student is not on-task, she will change the method of instruction accordingly. She may change from a teacher-directed approach to a more interactive approach. Questioning will increase in order to increase the participation of the students. If appropriate, the teacher will introduce manipulative materials to the lesson. In addition, teachers may switch to a cooperative group activity, thereby removing the responsibility of instruction from the teacher and putting it on the students.

29. **Curriculum mapping is an effective strategy because it...**
    (Rigorous) (Skill 5.1)

    A.   Provides an orderly sequence to instruction

    B.   Provides lesson plans for teachers to use and follow

    C.   Ties the curriculum into instruction

    D.   Provides a clear map so all students receive the same instruction across all classes

Answer: A. Provides an orderly sequence to instruction

Curriculum mapping is a strategy used to tie the actual curriculum with the support materials (text books) being utilized to support the teaching of said curriculum. Mapping is usually done to the month or quarter and provides a logical sequence to instruction so that all necessary skills and topics are covered in an appropriate fashion.

30. **Which of the following is the correct term for the alignment of the curriculum across all grades K-12?**
    (Rigorous) (Skill 5.1)

    A.   Data Based Decision Making

    B.   Curriculum Mapping

    C.   Vertical Integration

    D.   Curriculum Alignment

Answer: C. Vertical Integration

Curriculum mapping is the process of taking the curriculum and deciding when the information needs to be taught throughout the school year. Curriculum alignment involves the process of connecting the curriculum to something else (typically standards) to ensure all areas are being taught. Vertical integration is the process of ensuring that the curriculum flows in an appropriate manner from the lowest levels to the highest levels in a logical and responsible manner.

31. **When creating and selecting materials for instruction, teachers should complete which of the following steps:**
    (Average Rigor) (Skill 5.1)

    A.   Relevant to the prior knowledge of the students

    B.   Allow for a variation of learning styles

    C.   Choose alternative teaching strategies

    D.   All of the above

Answer: D. All of the above

It is imperative that when creating and selecting materials for instruction that teachers consider many different factors. This makes the planning for instruction a difficult and somewhat time consuming process. There are numerous factors which must always be balanced in order to deliver the most appropriate and beneficial instruction to students.

32. **When considering the development of the curriculum, which of the following accurately describes the four factors which need to be considered?**
    (Rigorous) (Skill 5.1)

    A.   Alignment, Scope, Sequence, and Design

    B.   Assessment, Instruction, Design, and Sequence

    C.   Data, Alignment, Correlation, and Score

    D.   Alignment, Sequence, Design and Assessment

Answer: A. Alignment, Scope, Sequence, and Design

When developing curriculum, it is important to first start with alignment. Alignment to state, national or other standards is the first step. Next, the scope of the curriculum involves looking at the amount of material covered within a grade level or subject. Next, the sequence of material needs to be considered. Finally, it is important to look at the design of the units individually from beginning to end.

33. **What should be considered when evaluating textbooks for content?** *(Average Rigor) (Skill 5.3)*

    A.   Type of print used

    B.   Number of photos used

    C.   Free of cultural stereotyping

    D.   Outlines at the beginning of each chapter

Answer: C. Free of cultural stereotyping.

While textbook writers and publishers have responded to the need to be culturally diverse in recent years, a few texts are still being offered that don't meet these standards. When teachers have an opportunity to be involved in choosing textbooks, they can be watchdogs for the community in keeping the curriculum free of matter that reinforces bigotry and discrimination.

34. **What are critical elements of instructional process?** *(Average Rigor) (Skill 5.4)*

    A.   Content, goals, teacher needs

    B.   Means of getting money to regulate instruction

    C.   Content, materials, activities, goals, learner needs

    D.   Materials, definitions, assignments

Answer: C Content, materials, activities, goals, learner needs.

Goal-setting is a vital component of the instructional process. The teacher will, of course, have overall goals for her class, both short-term and long-term. However, perhaps even more important than that is the setting of goals that take into account the individual learner's needs, background, and stage of development. Making an educational program child-centered involves building on the natural curiosity children bring to school, and asking children what they want to learn. Student-centered classrooms contain not only textbooks, workbooks, and literature but also rely heavily on a variety of audiovisual equipment and computers. There are tape recorders, language masters, filmstrip projectors, and laser disc players to help meet the learning styles of the students. Planning for instructional activities entails identification or selection of the activities the teacher and students will engage in during a period of instruction.

35. **What would improve planning for instruction?**
    (Average Rigor) (Skill 5.4)

    A.   Describe the role of the teacher and student

    B.   Evaluate the outcomes of instruction

    C.   Rearrange the order of activities

    D.   Give outside assignments

Answer is: B. Evaluate the outcomes of instruction.

Important as it is to plan content, materials, activities, goals taking into account learner needs and to base what goes on in the classroom on the results of that planning, it makes no difference if students are not able to demonstrate improvement in the skills being taught. An important part of the planning process is for the teacher to constantly adapt all aspects of the curriculum to what is actually happening in the classroom. Planning frequently misses the mark or fails to allow for unexpected factors. Evaluating the outcomes of instruction regularly and making adjustments accordingly will have a positive impact on the overall success of a teaching methodology.

36. The teacher states that the lesson the students will be engaged in will consist of a review of the material from the previous day, demonstration of the scientific of an electronic circuit, and small group work on setting up an electronic circuit. What has the teacher demonstrated?
(Rigorous) (Skill 5.4)

   A. The importance of reviewing

   B. Giving the general framework for the lesson to facilitate learning

   C. Giving students the opportunity to leave if they are not interested in the lesson

   D. Providing momentum for the lesson

Answer: B. Giving the general framework for the lesson to facilitate learning.

If children know where they're going, they're more likely to be engaged in getting there. It's important to give them a road map whenever possible for what is coming in their classes.

37. Which of the following describes why it is important and necessary for teachers to be able to analyze data on their students?
(Rigorous) (Skill 5.4)

   A. To provide appropriate instruction

   B. To make instructional decisions

   C. To communicate and determine instructional progress

   D. All of the above

Answer: D. All of the above

Especially in today's high stakes environment, it is critical teachers have a complete understanding of the process involved in examining student data in order to make instructional decisions, prepare lessons, determine progress, and report progress to stakeholders.

38. The teacher states, "We will work on the first page of vocabulary words. On the second page we will work on the structure and meaning of the words. We will go over these together and then you will write out the answers to the exercises on your own. I will be circulating to give help if needed". What is this an example of?
(Rigorous) (Skill 5.4)

    A.   Evaluation of instructional activity

    B.   Analysis of instructional activity

    C.   Identification of expected outcomes

    D.   Pacing of instructional activity

Answer: B. Analysis of instructional activity

The successful teacher carefully plans all activities to foresee any difficulties in executing the plan. This also assures that the directions being given to students will be clear, avoiding any misunderstanding.

39. If teachers attend to content, instructional materials, activities, learner needs, and goals in instructional planning, what could be an outcome?
(Rigorous) (Skill 5.4)

    A.   Planning for the next year

    B.   Effective classroom performance

    C.   Elevated test scores on standardized tests

    D.   More student involvement

Answer: B. Effective classroom performance

Another outcome will be teacher satisfaction in a job well-done and in the performance of her students. Her days will have far fewer disruptions and her classroom will be easy to manage.

40. **What is one component of the instructional planning model that must be given careful evaluation?**
(Rigorous) (Skill 5.5)

    A.   Students' prior knowledge and skills

    B.   The script the teacher will use in instruction

    C.   Future lesson plans

    D.   Parent participation

Answer: A. Students' prior knowledge and skills.

The teacher will, of course, have certain expectations regarding where the students will be physically and intellectually when he/she plans for a new class. However, there will be wide variations in the actual classroom. If he/she doesn't make the extra effort to understand where there are deficiencies and where there are strengths in the individual students, the planning will probably miss the mark, at least for some members of the class. This can be obtained through a review of student records, by observation, and by testing.

41. **What steps are important in the review of subject matter in the classroom?**
    (Rigorous) (Skill 5.5)

    A.   A lesson-initiating review, topic and a lesson-end review

    B.   A preview of the subject matter, an in-depth discussion, and a lesson-end review

    C.   A rehearsal of the subject matter and a topic summary within the lesson

    D.   A short paragraph synopsis of the previous day's lesson and a written review at the end of the lesson

Answer: A. A lesson-initiating review, topic, and a lesson-end review.

The effective teacher utilizes all three of these together with comprehension checks to make sure the students are processing the information. Lesson-end reviews are restatements (by the teacher or teacher and students) of the content of discussion at the end of a lesson. Subject matter retention increases when lessons include an outline at the beginning of the lesson and a summary at the end of the lesson. This type of structure is utilized in successful classrooms.
Moreover, when students know what is coming next, and what is expected of them, they feel more a part of their learning environment and deviant behavior is lessened.

42. **Which of the following is true about "readiness to learn?"**
    (Rigorous) (Skill 5.5)

    A.   It is possible to assess each student's readiness for each lesson.

    B.   The concept of readiness is a not a developmentally based phenomenon.

    C.   Readiness for subject area learning is also dependent on factors such as interest, motivation and attitude.

    D.   None of the above.

Answer: C. Readiness for subject area learning is also dependent on factors such as interest, motivation and attitude.

Readiness for subject area learning is dependent not only on prior knowledge, but also on affective factors such as interest, motivation, and attitude. These factors are often more influential on student learning than the pre-existing cognitive base.

43. When planning instruction, which of the following is an organizational tool to help ensure you are providing a well balanced set of objectives?
(Rigorous) (Skill 5.5)

    A.   Using taxonomy to develop objectives

    B.   Determining prior knowledge skill levels

    C.   Determining readiness levels

    D.   Ensuring you meet the needs of diverse learners

Answer: A. Using taxonomy to develop objectives

The use of taxonomy, such as Bloom's, allows teachers to ensure the students are receiving instruction at a variety of different levels. It is important students are able to demonstrate skills and knowledge at a variety of different levels.

44. Mr. Garcia is a math coach within his building. He is the only math coach in his building and in fact within his district. Mr. Garcia believes it is imperative he seek out the support of colleagues to work in a more collaborative manner. Which of the following would be an appropriate step for him to take?
(Rigorous) (Skill 5.7)

    A.   Collaborating with other teachers in his building regardless of their skill level knowledge in his area

    B.   Asking for the administration to find colleagues with which he can collaborate

    C.   Joining a professional organization such as the NCTM

    D.   Searching the internet for possible collaboration opportunities

Answer: C. Joining a professional organization such as the NCTM

Joining a professional organization, such as NCTM would provide Mr. German with the ability to learn and update his own knowledge specifically in his field of study and also open up the opportunity for him to interact with colleagues in his field from across the country.

45. **In the past, teaching has been viewed as _____ while in more current society it has been viewed as _____.**
    (Rigorous) (Skill 5.7)

    A.   Isolating….collaborative

    B.   Collaborative….isolating

    C.   Supportive…..isolating

    D.   Isolating…. Supportive

Answer: A. Isolating….collaborative

In the past, teachers often walked into their own classrooms and closed the door. They were not involved in any form of collaboration and were responsible for only the students within their classrooms. However, in today's more modern schools, teachers work in collaborative teams and are responsible for all of the children in a school setting.

46. **How are standardized tests useful in assessment?**
    (Average Rigor) (Skill 6.1)

    A.   For teacher evaluation

    B.   For evaluation of the administration

    C.   For comparison from school to school

    D.   For comparison to the population on which the test was normed

Answer: D. For comparison to the population on which the test was normed.

While the efficacy of the standardized tests that are being used nationally has come under attack recently, they are, actually the only device for comparing where an individual student stands with a wide range of peers. They also provide a measure for a program or a school to evaluate how their own students are doing as compared to the populace at large. Even so, they should not be the only measure upon which decisions are made or evaluations drawn. There are many other instruments for measuring student achievement that the teacher needs to consult and take into account.

47.   Which of the following is NOT used in evaluating test items?
        (Rigorous) (Skill 6.1)

        A.   Student feedback

        B.   Content validity

        C.   Reliability

        D.   Ineffective coefficient

Answer: D Ineffective coefficient.

The purpose for testing the students is to determine the extent to which the instructional objectives have been met. Therefore, the test items must be constructed to achieve the desired outcome from the students. Gronlund and Linn advise that effective tests begin with a test plan that includes the instructional objectives and subject matter to be tested, as well as the emphasis each item should have. Having a test plan will result in valid interpretation of student achievement.

48.   **How will students have a fair chance to demonstrate what they know on a test?**
        (Average Rigor) (Skill 6.2)

        A.   The examiner has strictly enforced rules for taking the test

        B.   The examiner provides a comfortable setting free of distractions and positively encourages the students

        C.   The examiner provides frequent stretch breaks to the students

        D.   The examiner stresses the importance of the test to the overall grade

Answer: B. The examiner provides a comfortable setting free of distractions and positively encourages the students.

Taking a test is intimidating to students at best. In addition, some students are unable to focus when there are distractions. Feeling that the teacher is on their side helps students relax and truly demonstrate what they have learned on a test.

49. **What is an example of formative feedback?**
    (Average Rigor) (Skill 6.2)

    A. The results of an intelligence test

    B. Correcting the tests in small groups

    C. Verbal behavior that expresses approval of a student response to a test item

    D. Scheduling a discussion prior to the test

Answer: C Verbal behavior that expresses approval of a student response to a test item.

Standardized testing is currently under great scrutiny but educators agree that any test that serves as a means of gathering and interpreting information about children's learning and which can provide accurate, helpful input for nurturing children's further growth is acceptable. All testing must be formative in nature. Formative evaluation is the basic, everyday kind of assessment that teachers continually do to understand students' growth and to help them learn further.

50. **What does the validity of a test refer to?**
    (Easy) (Skill 6.2)

    A. Its consistency

    B. Its usefulness

    C. Its accuracy

    D. The degree of true scores it provides

Answer: B. Its usefulness

The Joint technical standards for educational and psychological testing (APA, AERA, NCME, 1985) states: "Validity is the most important consideration in test evaluation. The concept refers to the appropriateness, meaningfulness and usefulness of the specific inferences made from test scores. Test validation is the process of accumulating evidence to support such inferences. A variety of inferences may be made from scores produced by a given test, and there are many ways of accumulating evidence to support any particular inference. Validity, however, is a unitary concept. Although evidence may be accumulated in many ways, validity always refers to the degree to which that evidence supports the inferences that are made from test scores."

51.   **Safeguards against bias and discrimination in the assessment of children include:**
        (Average Rigor) (Skill 6.2)

    A.   The testing of a child in standard English

    B.   The requirement for the use of one standardized test

    C.   The use of evaluative materials in the child's native language or other mode of communication

    D.   All testing performed by a certified, licensed, psychologist

Answer: C. The use of evaluative materials in the child's native language or other mode of communication

The law requires that the child be evaluated in his native language, or mode of communication. The idea that a licensed psychologist evaluates the child does not meet the criteria if it is not done in the child's normal mode of communication.

52.   **When a teacher wants to utilize an assessment which is subjective in nature, which of the following is the most effective method for scoring?**
        (Easy) (Skill 4.6)

    A.   Rubric

    B.   Checklist

    C.   Alternative Assessment

    D.   Subjective measures should not be utilized

Answer: A. Rubric

Rubrics are the most effective tool for assessing items which can be considered subjective. They provide the students with a clearer picture of teacher expectations and provide the teacher with a more consistent method of comparing this type of assignment.

53. **What is an effective way to prepare students for testing?**
    (Average Rigor) (Skill 6.4)

    A.   Minimize the importance of the test

    B.   Orient the students to the test, telling them of the purpose, how the results will be used and how it is relevant to them

    C.   Use the same format for every test are given

    D.   Have them construct an outline to study from

Answer: B. Orient the students to the test, telling them of the purpose, how the results will be used and how it is relevant to them.

If a test is to be an accurate measure of achievement, it must test the information, not the format of the test itself. If students know ahead of time what the test will be like, why they are taking it, what the teacher will do with the results, and what it has to do with them, the exercise is more likely to result in a true measure of what they've learned.

54. **Discovery learning is to inquiry as direct instruction is to...**
    (Rigorous) (Skill 7.1)

    A.   Scripted lessons

    B.   Well-developed instructions

    C.   Clear instructions which eliminate all misinterpretations

    D.   Creativity of teaching

Answer: C. Clear instructions which eliminate all misinterpretations

Direct instruction is a technique which relies on carefully well developed instructions and lessons which eliminate misinterpretations. In this manner, all students have the opportunity to acquire and learn the skills presented to the students. This approach limits teacher creativity to some extent, but has a good solid research based following with much ability to replicate its results.

55. **What do cooperative learning methods all have in common?**
(Average Rigor) (Skill 7.1)

    A.   Philosophy

    B.   Cooperative task/cooperative reward structures

    C.   Student roles and communication

    D.   Teacher roles

Answer: B. Cooperative task/cooperative reward structures.

Cooperative learning situations, as practiced in today's classrooms, grew out of searches conducted by several groups in the early 1970's. Cooperative learning situations can range from very formal applications such as STAD (Student Teams-Achievement Divisions) and CIRC (Cooperative Integrated Reading and Composition) to less formal groupings known variously as "group investigation," "learning together," and "discovery groups." Cooperative learning as a general term is now firmly recognized and established as a teaching and learning technique in American schools. Since cooperative learning techniques are so widely diffused in the schools, it is necessary to orient students in the skills by which cooperative learning groups can operate smoothly, and thereby enhance learning. Students who cannot interact constructively with other students will not be able to take advantage of the learning opportunities provided by the cooperative learning situations and will furthermore deprive their fellow students of the opportunity for cooperative learning.

56. **The use of technology in the classroom allows for...**
(Easy) (Skill 7.1)

    A.   More complex lessons

    B.   Better delivery of instruction

    C.   Variety of instruction

    D.   Better ability to meet more individual student needs

Answer: D. Better ability to meet more individual student needs

The utilization of technology provides the teacher with the opportunity to incorporate more than one learning style into a lesson. In this way, the teacher is better able to meet the individual needs of his/her students.

57. **When asking questions of students it is important to...**
(Easy) (Skill 7.3)

    A.   Use questions the students can answer

    B.   Provide numerous questions

    C.   Provide questions at various levels

    D.   Provide only a limited about of questions

Answer: C. Provide questions at various levels

Providing questions at various levels is essential to encourage deeper thinking and reflective thought processes.

58. **Which of following is <u>not</u> the role of the teacher in the instructional process?**
(Average Rigor) (Skill 7.5)

    A.   Instructor

    B.   Coach

    C.   Facilitator

    D.   Follower

Answer: D. Follower

The teacher demonstrates a variety of roles within the classroom. Teachers, however, should not be followers. They must balance all of their roles in an efficient way to ensure that instruction is delivered to meet the needs of his/her students.

59. **What do cooperative learning methods all have in common?**
(Average Rigor) (Skill 7.6)

    A.   Philosophy

    B.   Cooperative task/cooperative reward structures

    C.   Student roles and communication

    D.   Teacher roles

Answer: B. Cooperative task/cooperative reward structures.

Cooperative learning situations, as practiced in today's classrooms, grew out of searches conducted by several groups in the early 1970's. Cooperative learning situations can range from very formal applications such as STAD (Student Teams-Achievement Divisions) and CIRC (Cooperative Integrated Reading and Composition) to less formal groupings known variously as "group investigation," "learning together," and "discovery groups." Cooperative learning as a general term is now firmly recognized and established as a teaching and learning technique in American schools. Since cooperative learning techniques are so widely diffused in the schools, it is necessary to orient students in the skills by which cooperative learning groups can operate smoothly, and thereby enhance learning. Students who cannot interact constructively with other students will not be able to take advantage of the learning opportunities provided by the cooperative learning situations and will furthermore deprive their fellow students of the opportunity for cooperative learning.

60. **Which of the following is an accurate description of ESL students?**
    (Easy) (Skill 8.5)

    A.   Remedial students

    B.   Exceptional education students

    C.   Are not a homogeneous group

    D.   Feel confident in communicating in English when with their peers

Answer: C. Are not a homogeneous group.

Because ESL students are often grouped in classes that take a different approach to teaching English than those for native speakers, it's easy to assume that they all present with the same needs and characteristics. Nothing could be further from the truth, even in what they need when it comes to learning English. It's important that their backgrounds and personalities be observed just as with native speakers. It was very surprising several years ago when Vietnamese children began arriving in American schools with little training in English and went on to excel in their classes, often even beyond their American counterparts. In many schools, there were Vietnamese merit scholars in the graduating classes.

61. **What is an effective way to help a non-English speaking student succeed in class?**
    (Rigorous) (Skill 8.5)

    A.   Refer the child to a specialist

    B.   Maintain an encouraging, success-oriented atmosphere

    C.   Help them assimilate by making them use English exclusively

    D.   Help them cope with the content materials you presently use

Answer: B. Maintain an encouraging, success-oriented atmosphere.

Anyone who is in an environment where his language is not the standard one feels embarrassed and inferior. The student who is in that situation expects to fail. Encouragement is even more important for these students. They need many opportunities to succeed.

62. **Mrs. Grant is providing her students with many extrinsic motivators in order to increase their intrinsic motivation. Which of the following best explains this relationship?**
(Rigorous) (Skill 9.2)

A.   This is a good relationship and will increase intrinsic motivation

B.   The relationship builds animosity between the teacher and the students

C.   Extrinsic motivation does not in itself help to build intrinsic motivation

D.   There is no place for extrinsic motivation in the classroom

Answer: C. Extrinsic motivation does not in itself help to build intrinsic motivation

There are some cases where it is necessary to utilize extrinsic motivation; however, the use of extrinsic motivation is not alone a strategy to use to build intrinsic motivation. Intrinsic motivation comes from within the student themselves, while extrinsic motivation comes from outside parties.

63. **What has been established to increase student originality, intrinsic motivation, and higher order thinking skills?**
(Rigorous) (Skill 9.2)

A.   Classroom climate

B.   High expectations

C.   Student choice

D.   Use of authentic learning opportunities

Answer: C. Student choice

While all of the descriptors are good attributes for students to demonstrate, it has been shown through research that providing student choice can increase all of the described factors.

64.   **How can the teacher establish a positive climate in the classroom?**
       (Average Rigor) (Skill 9.4)

      A.   Help students see the unique contributions of individual differences

      B.   Use whole group instruction for all content areas

      C.   Help students divide into cooperative groups based on ability

      D.   Eliminate teaching strategies that allow students to make choices

Answer: A. Help students see the unique contributions of individual differences.

In the first place, an important purpose of education is to prepare students to live successfully in the real world, and this is an important insight and understanding for them to take into that world. In the second place, the most fertile learning environment is one in which all viewpoints and backgrounds are respected and where everyone has equal respect.

65.   **How can student misconduct be redirected at times?**
       (Average Rigor) (Skill 9.5)

      A.   The teacher threatens the students

      B.   The teacher assigns detention to the whole class

      C.   The teacher stops the activity and stares at the students

      D.   The teacher effectively handles changing from one activity to another

Answer: D. The teacher effectively handles changing from one activity to another.

Appropriate verbal techniques include a soft non-threatening voice void of undue roughness, anger, or impatience regardless of whether the teacher is instructing, providing student alerts, or giving a behavior reprimand. Verbal techniques that may be effective in modifying student behavior include simply stating the student's name, explaining briefly and succinctly what the student is doing that is inappropriate and what the student should be doing. Verbal techniques for reinforcing behavior include both encouragement and praise delivered by the teacher. In addition, for verbal techniques to positively affect student behavior and learning, the teacher must give clear, concise directives while implying her warmth toward the students.

66. **What is one way of effectively managing student conduct?**
    (Average Rigor) (Skill 9.6)

    A.   State expectations about behavior

    B.   Let students discipline their peers

    C.   Let minor infractions of the rules go unnoticed

    D.   Increase disapproving remarks

Answer: A. State expectations about behavior.

The effective teacher demonstrates awareness of what the entire class is doing and is in control of the behavior of all students even when the teacher is working with only a small group of the children. In an attempt to prevent student misbehaviors the teacher makes clear, concise statements about what is happening in the classroom directing attention to content and the students' accountability for their work rather than focusing the class on the misbehavior. It is also effective for the teacher to make a positive statement about the appropriate behavior that is observed. If deviant behavior does occur, the effective teacher will specify who the deviant is, what he or she is doing wrong, and why this is unacceptable conduct or what the proper conduct would be. This can be a difficult task to accomplish as the teacher must maintain academic focus and flow while addressing and desisting misbehavior. The teacher must make clear, brief statements about the expectations without raising his/her voice and without disrupting instruction.

67. **What is a sample of an academic transition signal?**
    (Average Rigor) (Skill 9.6)

    A. "How do clouds form?"

    B. "Today we are going to study clouds."

    C. "We have completed today's lesson."

    D. "That completes the description of cumulus clouds. Now we will look at the description of cirrus clouds."

Answer: D. "That completes the description of cumulus clouds. Now we will look at the description of cirrus clouds."

Transitions are language bridges between one topic and another. The teacher should thoughtfully plan transitions when several topics are going to be presented in one lesson to be sure that students are carried along. Without transitions, sometimes students are still focused on a previous topic and are lost in the discussion.

68. **A parent has left an angry message on the teacher's voicemail. The message relates to a concern about a student and is directed at the teacher. The teacher should:**
    (Average Rigor) (Skill 10.1)

    A. Call back immediately and confront the parent

    B. Cool off, plan what to discuss with the parent, then call back

    C. Question the child to find out what set off the parent

    D. Ignore the message

Answer: B. Cool off, plan what to discuss with the parent, then call back

It is professional for a teacher to keep her head in the face of emotion and respond to an angry parent in a calm and objective manner. The teacher should give herself time to cool off and plan the conversation with the parent with the purpose of understanding the concern and resolving it, rather than putting the parent in their place. Above all the teacher should remember that parent-teacher interactions should aim to benefit the student.

69.   Mr. Brown wishes to improve his parent communication skills.
       Which of the following is a strategy he can utilize to accomplish this
       goal?
       (Easy) (Skill 10.1)

       A.   Hold parent-teacher conferences

       B.   Send home positive notes

       C.   Have parent nights where the parents are invited into his classroom

       D.   All of the above

Answer: D. All of the above

Increasing parent communication skills is important for teachers. All of the listed
strategies are methods a teacher can utilize to increase his skills.

70.   Tommy is a student in your class, his parents are deaf. Tommy is
       struggling with math and you want to contact the parents to discuss
       the issues. How should you proceed?
       (Easy) (Skill 10.1)

       A.   Limit contact due to the parent's inability to hear

       B.   Use a TTY phone to communicate with the parents

       C.   Talk to your administrator to find an appropriate interpreter to help
             you communicate with the parents personally

       D.   Both B and C but not A

Answer: D. Both B and C but not A

You should never avoid communicating with parents for any reason; instead you
should find strategies to find an effective way to communicate in various
methods, just as you would with any other student in your classroom.

71. **When communicating with parents for whom English is not the primary language you should:**
(Easy) (Skill 10.1)

    A.   Provide materials whenever possible in their native language

    B.   Use an interpreter

    C.   Provide the same communication as you would to native English speaking parents

    D.   All of the above

Answer: D. All of the above

When communicating with non English speaking parents it is important to treat them as you would any other parent and utilize any means necessary to ensure they have the ability to participate in their child's educational process.

72. **Marco's mother is quite irate. She calls in and leaves a message on your voicemail. After listening to the voicemail, which of the following is the most appropriate response for you to make?**
(Easy) (Skill 10.1)

    A.   Have the principal return the call

    B.   Ask Marco's mother to come into school for a meeting

    C.   Ignore the phone call

    D.   Return the call and discuss the issue over the phone

Answer: B. Ask Marco's mother to come into school for a meeting

It is best to discuss difficult situations in person rather than over the phone. First, it is sometimes helpful to involve other parties, which is often difficult to do on the phone. Second, the personal connection allows you to show appropriate documentation or other information which cannot be done over the phone. Finally, having other parties present can help to avoid, he said/ she said situations at a later time.

73. **Which of the following is NOT a sound educational practice for expanding the professional development opportunities for teachers?**
(Rigorous) (Skill 11.1)

  A. Looking at multiple methods of classroom management strategies

  B. Training teachers in understanding and applying multiple assessment formats and implementations in curriculum and instruction

  C. Having the students complete professional development assessments on a regular basis

  D. Teaching teachers how to disaggregate student data in improving instruction and curriculum implementation for student academic equity and access

Answer: C. Having the students complete professional development assessments on a regular basis

Giving teachers tests on a regular basis, while providing information on what knowledge they may have does not expand the professional development opportunities for teachers.

74. **What would happen if a school utilized an integrated approach to professional development?**
(Rigorous) (Skill 11.1)

  A. All stakeholders' needs are addressed

  B. Teachers and administrators are on the same page

  C. High quality programs for students are developed

  D. Parents drive the curriculum and instruction

Answer: C. High quality programs for students are developed

The implementation of an integrated approach to professional development is a critical component to ensuring success of programs for students. It involves teachers, parents and other community members working together to develop appropriate programs to ensure students are receiving the necessary instruction to be successful in the future workforce.

75. **The child study team is the first line of defense for a teacher when…** *(Rigorous) (Skill 11.3)*

    A.   A student is in special education

    B.   A student is struggling within the regular curriculum

    C.   A principal feels a teacher needs support in delivering instruction

    D.   A student needs services outside of the school district

Answer: B. A student is struggling within the regular curriculum

All schools have guidelines for receiving this assistance especially since the implementation of the Americans with Disabilities Act. The first step in securing help is for the teacher to approach the school's administration or exceptional education department for direction in attaining special services or resources for qualifying students. Many schools have a committee designated for addressing these needs such as a Child Study Team or Core Team. These teams are made up of both regular and exceptional education teachers, school psychologists, guidance counselors, and administrators. The particular student's classroom teacher usually has to complete some initial paper work and will need to do some behavioral observations.

76. **A 16 year-old girl who has been looking sad writes an essay in which the main protagonist commits suicide. You overhear her talking about suicide. What do you do?**
   (Average Rigor) (Skill 11.3)

   A.   Report this immediately to school administration, talk to the girl, letting her know you will talk to her parents about it

   B.   Report this immediately to authorities

   C.   Report this immediately to school administration. Make your own report to authorities if required by protocol in your school. Do nothing else

   D.   Just give the child some extra attention, as it may just be that's all she's looking for

Answer: C. Report this immediately to school administration. Make your own report to authorities if required by protocol in your school. Do nothing else.

A child who is suicidal is beyond any help that can be offered in a classroom. The first step is to report the situation to administration. If your school protocol calls for it, the situation should also be reported to authorities.

77. Sandy, a student with identified special needs, requires a change in her educational placement. Sandy's parents do not agree with the school system on what is the best educational placement for Sandy. Which of the following is one possible course of action the school system can take?
    (Rigorous) (Skill 11.3)

    A.   Due Process

    B.   Hold an IEP team meeting

    C.   Ignore the parent's wishes

    D.   File suit against the parents

Answer: B. Hold an IEP team meeting

With the updates in the federal laws governing special education, it is important to constantly check with the specific laws for your region and district. Typically, the school cannot file a due process suit against parents. This is recourse only available to parents. Holding an IEP team meeting or perhaps a mediation with the parents is the most beneficial and meaningful attempt to resolve issues. Optimal conditions for a disabled student's education exist when teachers, school administrators, special education professionals and parents/guardians work together to design and execute the IEP.

78. **Which of the following could be an example of a situation which could have an effect on a student's learning and academic progress?**
(Average Rigor) (Skill 11.3)

   A.   Relocation

   B.   Abuse

   C.   Both of the above

   D.   Neither of the above

Answer: C. Both of the above

There are an unlimited amount of situations which can affect a student's learning. Teachers need to keep in mind this when teaching. Students are whole people and just as stress affects us as adults, children experience the same feelings. They usually do not have the same tool box that adults have to deal with the feelings and may require some additional guidance.

79. **You receive a phone call from a person who indicates she is now tutoring a student in your class. She would like you to provide an overview of the academic areas which the student is having difficulties. What is the first thing you should do?**
(Rigorous) (Skill 11.5)

   A.   Find a time and talk with the tutor about issues you see within the classroom

   B.   Call the parents

   C.   Put together a packet of information to share with the tutor

   D.   Offer to invite the tutor in to have a discussion and observe the child

Answer: B. Call the parents

Before you share any information with anyone about a student, you should always secure parental permission in writing.

80. **The IEP should contain all of the following except...**
     (Average Rigor) (Skill 11.3)

  A. Grades

  B. Transition Plans

  C. Current Performance

  D. Service

Answer: A. Grades

By law, the IEP must include certain information about the child and the educational program designed to meet his or her unique needs.

  • Current performance. The IEP must state how the child is currently performing in school (known as present levels of educational performance). This information usually comes from evaluation results such as classroom tests and assignments, individual tests given to decide eligibility for services or during reevaluation, and observations made by parents, teachers, related service providers, and other school staff. The statement about "current performance" includes how the child's disability affects his or her involvement and progress in the general curriculum.

  • Annual goals. These are goals that the child can reasonably accomplish in a year. The goals are broken down into short-term objectives or benchmarks. Goals may be academic, social or behavioral, relate to physical needs, or address other educational needs. The goals must be measurable.

  • Special education and related services. The IEP must list the special education and related services to be provided to the child or on behalf of the child. This includes supplementary aids and services that the child needs. It also includes modifications (changes) to the program or supports for school personnel--such as training or professional development--that will be provided to assist the child.

  • Participation with non disabled children. The IEP must explain the extent (if any) to which the child will not participate with non disabled children in the regular class and other school activities.

  • Participation in state and district-wide tests. The IEP must state what modifications in the administration of these tests the child will need. If a test is not appropriate for the child, the IEP must state why the test is not appropriate and how the child will be tested instead.

  • Dates and places. The IEP must state when services will begin, how often they will be provided, where they will be provided, and how long they will last.

- Transition service needs. Beginning when the child is age 14 (or younger, if appropriate), the IEP must address (within the applicable parts of the IEP) the courses the student needs to take to reach his or her post-school goals. A statement of transition services needs must also be included in each of the child's subsequent IEPs.
- Needed transition services. Beginning when the child is age 16 (or younger, if appropriate), the IEP must state what transition services are needed to help the child prepare for leaving school.
- Age of majority. Beginning at least one year before the child reaches the age of majority, the IEP must include a statement that the student has been told of any rights that will transfer to him or her at the age of majority (where applicable).
- Measuring progress. The IEP must state how the child's progress will be measured and how parents/legal guardians will be informed of that progress

SAMPLE CONSTRUCTED-RESPONSE MODULES

The content covered by the modules described below is assessed through the constructed-response component of the Oklahoma Professional Teaching Examination. The test consists of three constructed response modules, and examples are provided below.

CRITICAL ANALYSIS MODULE: Learners and the Learning Environment

This module requires candidates to construct written responses that demonstrate an understanding of aspects of professional knowledge as described in Subarea I. Assignments and responses for this module will relate to Competencies 1.0, 2.0, 3.0, and/or 4.0 of the test framework.

This component of the assessment requires candidates to exercise critical thinking skills to analyze educational issues related to learners and the learning environment and present their own opinions in a coherent and convincing way.

For example, the candidate is presented with a brief summary of a contemporary educational issue or topic (e.g., student development patterns, theories of learning, motivational techniques). The candidate responds in writing by presenting his or her own point of view on the topic and supporting that position with reasoned arguments and appropriate examples.

SAMPLE ASSIGNMENT:

You will now be asked to analyze and discuss an educational issue related to Subarea 1 of the OPTE test framework, "Learners and the Learning Environment"

Respond to the following Critical Analysis Module Assignment:

Student Learning: Standards-Driven or Project-Based?

In an age of accountability for student learning, many educators assume that sticking to standards and ensuring that each standard is covered explicitly is the safest and most prudent thing to do. However, there are still many educators that believe that standards can be covered, perhaps in a non-linear fashion, by engaging students in academic and cross-curricular projects. Those who believe that project-based instruction is more valuable suggest that students will enjoy their learning more and will still learn many important academic standards in the process. Those who believe that standards-driven learning is more valuable might argue that it is unfair to students to not cover each and every area that they will be tested on. They might also suggest that teaching standards in a linear fashion will provide greater clarity for students.

In a response written for an audience of teachers, use your knowledge of learners and the learning environment to analyze and discuss the issue of standards-driven and project-based teaching.

RESPONSE:

There is no doubt that students must be prepared based on state standards. However, when analyzing state standards, it is important to realize that while standards may look like a bunch of unconnected skills, they really do build upon one another and there is quite a bit of information that overlaps. In my first year as a high school Language Arts teacher, I know that it is important to focus both on standards as well as engaging, meaningful projects. I do not believe that a teacher would have to choose between the two approaches, standards-driven and project-based.

When evaluating what to teach and how to teach it, it is important first to ensure that what is being taught can be defended by the standards. Teachers must make sure that students learn what is required, as students are tested on that material. They are also expected to know that material as they progress to the next grade level.

However, not all students will learn at the same pace and in the same way. Furthermore, if a teacher were to simply "cover" the standards, students would have little context for understanding the material, and it certainly would not be very exciting. Students need to feel that what they are learning is important beyond passing tests. For that reason, developing lessons, units, and projects that take students' varied learning styles into account and draw upon real-world examples and issues will make learning more fun, and it will ensure that all students learn. However, such lessons, units, and projects should also be based on standards so that students have interesting, enjoyable, and student-centered ways of learning the information they are required to know. This method seems to be a more logical approach that combines the positives of both positions.

An example of combining these two approaches, based on a secondary Language Arts classroom, is the teaching of literature. For example, a particular standard might call for students to understand imagery in literature. Another standard might call for students to learn about specific eras in American literature. Another might call for students to learn how to write an analysis of literary techniques. If I were to teach based on standards-driven principles, I would teach all these skills out of context. Yet, if I were to focus simply on a project-based method, I might not hit any of these issues. However, if I were to have students engage in a project that focused on each of these areas and gave them choice in the way they work toward the final project, while giving specialized assistance to those who need it, students will get the opportunity to learn these skills, and they will more likely enjoy the process and learn at an appropriate pace.

Combining both approaches seems most logical. While many educators argue that standards-drive instruction is the only way to ensure that students are prepared for testing, doing so alone will provide little opportunity for students to learn in ways that are natural for them. On the other hand, while many educators are convinced that doing anything other than project-based instruction will be boring for students, not paying significant attention to standards will ensure that students are not prepared for the complex academic tasks they will be required to master.

EVALUATION:

The assignment asked the candidate to analyze two claims, both at odds with each other. One side, suggesting that standards-driven instruction is more appropriate, seemingly goes against the other side, project-based instruction. Yet the candidate wrote an essay that effectively found the best of both methods. The essay demonstrates a deep knowledge of student learning, as well as contemporary issues of curriculum and instruction. It demonstrated knowledge of student engagement and standards-based instruction. Although the essay did not ask for the candidate to demonstrate the best of both models, its strength lies in the fact that it does indeed show how both methods have some limitations as well as some strengths. Putting both together with a good curricular example was effective. This essay demonstrates strong knowledge of Subarea 1 of the OPTE framework.

STUDENT INQUIRY MODULE: Instruction and Assessment

This module requires candidates to construct written responses that demonstrate an understanding of aspects of professional knowledge as described in Subarea II. Assignments and responses for this module will relate to Competencies 5.0, 6.0, 7.0, 8.0, and/or 9.0 of the test framework.

This component of the assessment requires the candidate to apply general principles of teaching and learning in planning, delivering, and adapting instruction and assessment. For example, the candidate is presented with an instructional goal (e.g., fostering students' critical thinking skills, providing opportunities for students to explore a topic using a range of learning modes, helping students relate instructional content to their own experience). The candidate responds in writing by describing and evaluating instructional strategies and activities designed to help students attain that goal.

SAMPLE ASSIGNMENT:

You will now be asked to demonstrate your knowledge of Subarea II, Instruction and Assessment.

Respond to the following Student Inquiry Module assignment:

LEARNING GOAL: Students will learn and apply new information through the use of hands-on activities.

In a written response for an audience of teachers, identify a grade/age level and subject area for which you are prepared to teach, then use your knowledge of instruction and assessment to:

- Describe a "hands-on" activity or lesson that would help students to learn and apply new information.
- Explain why this "hands-on" activity or lesson would be helpful in teaching students new information.

RESPONSE:

For a second grade math lesson, I might end up teaching students about fractions. While fractions are difficult to learn about with just numbers, using manipulatives and hands-on activities, students will quickly understand the concept of fractions much faster. I would begin a series of lessons on fractions with a hands-on activity that would start with me modeling the activity. Then, students would work in groups to practice on their own.

The first step of this lesson would involve me at the overhead projector. I would draw a picture of a pie on the overhead and suggest that I was going to have five friends over to help me eat it. I would ask students, "So, how am I going to make sure everyone has the same amount of pie?" I would then start to draw lines all over the place—one piece would be very large, a few pieces would be quite small, and the last few would be regular pieces of pie. I would ask students if this looked right. Hopefully, they will say that the pieces are a variety of different sizes. I would then ask them to help me cut the pie so that everyone would have a similar-sized slice. I would end the activity by asking them how many slices I had of ONE pie. They should be able to say that we have six slices.

The next step would be to get the students into groups of three to four students. I would give them cut-outs of a variety of different items. The first would be a pizza. I would then ask them to determine how many slices they would need in order to make sure everyone got one similarly-sized slice. They would have to cut the pizza so that everyone gets the same sized slice. With another paper pizza, they would have to include leftovers for two friends. With yet another paper pizza, they would have to include leftover for each of them for the next day. After cutting out various-sized slices on each pizza, I would have them count up how many slices they got from each pizza.

The final step of this "hands-on" lesson would be to have them, in groups, show me what one-half a pizza would be. On each pizza, they would count up how many slices they have. This would go on and on until they understand that one-half or one-quarter could constitute a variety of numbers of slices depending how many slices were cut for each pizza.

This activity would help students learn the concept of fractions by giving them a practical, simple method of seeing fractions. They would understand that one pizza could have many different combinations of slices. Because they are the same sized pizzas, each one-half or one-quarter would constitute the same size, yet have different numbers of slices. They would be able to learn the concept by applying it with a simple hands-on activity that involves dividing something for friends and leftovers, something they are already familiar with. Overall, this is a fun, practical, and useful way to teach the very difficult concept of fractions.

EVALUATION:

This essay demonstrates a very good knowledge of "hands-on" activities in the teaching of math. It clearly shows how various concepts of instruction can be tailored for different learning styles and different instructional standards. The candidate shows a good working knowledge of the Subarea by demonstrating the importance of carefully designing a lesson in order to meet students' learning needs. The lesson is very clear, and directions are provided step-by-step. No element of instruction is left out. Furthermore, the essay ends with a very good overview of how this lesson would meet students' learning needs, and it argues convincingly for using hands-on methods to teach this concept. Finally, the candidate chose a topic for which hands-on instruction would be very appropriate.

TEACHER ASSIGNMENT MODULE: The Professional Environment

This module requires candidates to construct written responses that demonstrate an understanding of aspects of professional knowledge as described in Subarea III. Assignments and responses for this module will relate to Competencies 10.0, 11.0, 0012, and/or 0013 of the test framework.

This component of the assessment requires the candidate to reflect on and apply knowledge of the professional roles and responsibilities of the teacher. For example, the candidate is presented with a situation arising from an interaction with colleagues, parents/guardians, or community members and requiring some form of action. The candidate responds in writing by identifying and discussing important issues raised by the situation, describing an appropriate course of action, and explaining how the proposed action is likely to lead to a desirable outcome.

SAMPLE ASSIGNMENT:

In the following Teacher Assignment Module, you will be asked to use your knowledge of Subarea III of the OPTE test framework, "The Professional Environment."

Respond to the following Teacher Assignment Module assignment:

Half-way through the school year, a week after semester report cards are sent home, you get an email from a student's parent complaining that you gave her son low grades for no good reason. She suggests that she has heard nothing but complaints about your teaching and that if you were a better teacher, her son would not have such low grades. She wants to (a) meet with you and the principal together, (b) examine other students' grades to see how her son's grades compare, and (c) have you put together extra credit work so that her son can raise her grade.

In a written response to an audience of educators, use your knowledge of the professional environment to:

- Identify the important issues at stake in this scenario.
- Describe a plan of action you would take to remedy this problem.
- Explain why your plan would be effective in resolving the issue.

RESPONSE:

The primary concern in this scenario is the difference of opinion about the student's academic standing in the class. Obviously, the teacher felt that the student deserved a particular grade, and the parent believes that the grade should be higher. This is an issue of assessment, but it is also an issue of politics, parent-school relations, and legalities.

As a teacher, I would do whatever I could to be fair to all students, including the student under question. I would not immediately change the grade, nor would I ignore the parent's concern. In general, I would want to begin by collecting data on the issue, inform the principal, and appropriately interact with the parent. I would not, however, allow the parent to view other students' grades, as this would be illegal.

First, I would inform the principal that a concern has come up regarding a student's grade. I would let the principal know my plan for dealing with this, and I would suggest that a meeting may be necessary. Even though I would have to come back to the principal to discuss the issue in further detail later, I would simply want the principal to know that an incident has occurred so that he/she would be informed and so that I could document that I have gone through all the proper chains of command.

Second, I would do some investigation on my own grading practices, as well as the student's work. Because I would have documented progress and all grades carefully, as well as compiled portfolios of all my students' work, I would not have any problem in accessing the information I would need to determine if I had made an error in evaluation. While reviewing this information, I would document everything I find.

Third, I would collect all scoring guides, rubrics, assignments, and other materials that would explain how I evaluated students. I would make sure that I could see a clear documentation in my grading based on the criteria students were aware of when they completed the work.

Fourth, I would convene a meeting with the student's parent and the principal. Although I would bring my documentation, I would want to start by listening to the parent's concerns over her perceptions of my teaching. I would take those concerns seriously and write each one down to demonstrate respect. No matter what, I would review with the parent all the material I brought. However, I would want to end the meeting by offering a "win-win" solution. I would encourage the parent to work with me to determine how her son could get good grades for the next semester.

Of course, if I found an error in my evaluation, I would ensure that the grade be changed. However, under no circumstances would it be fair to offer extra credit to one student and not the others.

What this scenario tells me is that I would want to keep in constant contact with parents, particularly of students whose grades were low throughout the semester. While I would have to back-track in this scenario, I would ensure that in future semesters, I never let a student get to a low grade without first having conferences with the student and his/her parent. This scenario also suggests that evaluation is not just about grades. It's about ensuring that students have been properly prepared for what they will be assessed on. It's also about making sure that assessment is fair and utilized for the purpose of tracking students' progress. If, for example, some students' progress shows little growth, that would be a sign to me to deal with those issues immediately.

As a summary, my method of dealing with this scenario shows respect in the student and parent, yet it relies on careful methods of evaluation of student progress. It demonstrates that it is important to be courteous to parents and to keep principals informed of incidents. Documentation is also crucial in many ways so that students and parents can be assured that fairness will be applied in all aspects of a teacher's class.

EVALUATION:

This response offers a very detailed and comprehensive explanation of a strategy that could be followed for any disagreement about grades. What is most promising about this response is that it goes beyond the incident itself to show how respect, documentation, and full disclosure are important in the field of teaching. In many ways, it also demonstrates a careful process of applying fairness to the classroom.

STATE MAJOR COMPONENTS RETAINED AND CHANGES OF IDEA 2004

The second revision of IDEA occurred in 2004, IDEA was re-authorized as the Individuals with Disabilities Education Improvement Act of 2004 (IDEIA 2004) is commonly referred to as IDEA 2004. IDEA 2004 was effective July 1, 2005.

It was the intention to improve IDEA by adding the philosophy and understanding that special education students need preparation for further study beyond the high school setting by teaching compensatory methods. Accordingly, IDEA 2004 provided a close tie to PL 89-10, the Elementary and Special Education Act of 1965, and stated that students with special needs should have maximum access to the general curriculum. This was defined as the amount for an individual student to reach his fullest potential. Full inclusion was stated not to be the only option by which to achieve this, and specified that skills should be taught to compensate students later in life in cases where inclusion was not the best setting.

IDEA 2004 added a new requirement for special education teachers on the secondary level enforcing NCLBs "Highly Qualified" requirements in the subject area of their curriculum. The rewording in this part of IDEA states that they shall be "no less qualified" than teachers in the core areas.

Free and Appropriate Public Education (FAPE), was revised by mandating that students have maximum access to appropriate general education. Additionally, LRE placement for those students with disabilities must have the same school placement rights as those students who are not disabled. IDEA 2004 recognizes that due to the nature of some disabilities, appropriate education may vary in the amount of participation / placement in the general education setting.   For some students, FAPE will mean a choice as to the type of educational institution they attend (private school for example), any of which must provide the special education services deemed necessary for the student through the IEP.

The definition of Assistive technology devices was amended to exclude devices that are surgically implanted (i.e. cochlear implants), and clarified that students with assistive technology devices shall not be prevented from having special education services. Assistive technology devices may need to monitored by school personnel, but schools are not responsible for the implantation or replacement of such devices surgically. An example of this would be a cochlear implant.

The definition of Child with a disability is the term used for children ages 3-9 with a developmental delay now has been was changed to allow for the inclusion of Tourettes Syndrome.

IDEA 2004 recognized that all states must follow the National Instructional Materials Accessibility Standards which states that students who need materials in a certain form will get those at the same time their non-disabled peers receive their materials.   Teacher recognition of this standard is important.

Changes in Requirements for Evaluations

The clock/time allowance between the request for an initial evaluation and the determination if a disability is present may be requested has been changed to state the finding/determination must occur within 60 calendar days of the request. This is a significant change as previously it was interpreted to mean 60 school days. Parental consent is also required for evaluations and prior to the start of special education services.

No single assessment or measurement tool may now be used to determine special education qualification. Assessments and measurements used should be in language and form that will give the most accurate picture of the child's abilities.

IDEA 2004's recognized that there exists a disproportionate representation of minorities and bilingual students and that pre-service interventions that are scientifically based on early reading programs, positive behavioral interventions and support, and early intervening services) may prevent some of those children from needing special education services. This understanding has led to a child not being considered to have a disability if he/she has not had appropriate education in math or reading, nor shall a child be considered to have a disability if the reason for his/her delays is that English is a second language.

When determining a specific learning disability, the criteria may or may not use a discrepancy between achievement and intellectual ability but whether or not the child responds to scientific research-based intervention. In general, children who may not have been found eligible for special education (via testing) but are known to need services (via functioning, excluding lack of instruction) are still eligible for special education services. This change now allows input for evaluation to include state and local testing, classroom observation, academic achievement, and related developmental needs,

Changes in Requirements for IEPs

Individualized Education Plans (IEPS) continue to have multiple sections. One section, present levels, now addresses academic achievement and functional performance. Annual IEP goals must now address the same areas.

IEP goals should be aligned to state standards, thus short term objectives are not required on every IEP. Students with IEPs must not only participate in regular education programs to the full extent possible, they must show progress in those programs. This means that goals should be written to reflect academic progress.

For students who must participate in alternate assessment, there must be alignment to alternate achievement standards.

Significant change has been made in the definition of the IEP team as it now includes not less than 1 teacher from each of the areas of special education and regular education be present.

IDEA 2004 recognized that the amount of required paperwork placed upon teachers of students with disabilities should be reduced if possible, for this reason a pilot program has been developed in which some states will participate using multi-year IEPs. Individual student inclusion in this program will require consent by both the school and the parent.

XAMonline, INC. 21 Orient Ave. Melrose, MA 02176

Toll Free number 800-509-4128

TO ORDER Fax 781-662-9268 OR www.XAMonline.com

ARIZONA Teacher Certification -AEPA- 2008

PO#   Store/School:

Address 1:

Address 2 (Ship to other):

City, State Zip

 Credit card number_____-_____-_____-_____   expiration_____

EMAIL _____

PHONE   FAX

ISBN	TITLE	Qty	Retail	Total
978-1-58197-747-9	AEPA EARLY CHILDHOOD EDUCATION 36			
9781-58197-749-3	AEPA BASIC SKILLS 96, 97, 98			
978-1-58197-738-7	AEPA ELEMENTARY EDUCATION 01			
978-1-58197-703-5	AEPA ENGLISH 02			
978-1-58197-731-8	AEPA SOCIAL STUDIES 03			
978-1-58197-732-5	AEPA BIOLOGY 07			
978-1-58197-722-6	AEPA CHEMISTRY 08			
978-1-58197-748-6	AEPA PHYSICS 09			
978-1-58197-642-7	AEPA MIDDLE SCHOOL MATHEMATICS 37			
978-1-58197-641-0	AEPA MATHEMATICS 10			
978-1-58197-746-2	AEPA HEALTH 18			
978-1-58197-734-9	AEPA LIBRARY-EDUCATIONAL MEDIA 12			
978-1-58197-729-5	AEPA ART SAMPLE TEST 13			
978-1-58197-735-6	AEPA SPANISH 15			
978-1-58197-743-1	AEPA HISTORY 05			
978-1-58197-736-3	AEPA FRENCH SAMPLE TEST 16			
978-1-58197-739-4	AEPA SPECIAL EDUCATION - EMOTIONAL DISABILTIES 24			
978-1-58197-737-0	AEPA SPECIAL EDUCATION: CROSS-CATEGORY 22			
978-1-58197-745-5	AEPA CONSTITUTION OF THE UNITED STATES AND ARIZONA 33			
978-1-58197-740-0	AEPA POLITICAL SCIENCE/AMERICAN GOVERNMENT 06			
978-1-58197-291-7	AEPA PROFESSIONAL KNOWLEDGE - ELEMENTARY & SECONDARY 91, 92			
			SUBTOTAL	
	Ship 1 book $8.70, 2 books $11.00		Ship	$8.70
			TOTAL	

Printed in the United States
136562LV00001B/104/P

9 781581 972917